Guidance and Counselling for School Students

Guidance and Counselling for School Students

Dr. Ramesh Chaturvedi

CRESCENT
PUBLISHING CORPORATION

[*The responsibility for the facts stated, conclusions reached and plagiarism, if any, in this book is entirely that of the Author. And the Publisher bears no responsibility for them, whatsoever.*]

Guidance and Counselling for School Students

First Published : 2013

ISBN 81-8342-077-X

Published by :

CRESCENT PUBLISHING CORPORATION

4831/24, Prahlad Street,
Ansari Road, Darya Ganj,
New Delhi - 110002
Ph. : 23272541, 23257835
Fax : 91- 011- 23257835
e-mail : campusbooks@hotmail.com

Printed at :

Roshan Offset Printers

Delhi

Preface

In every school, school counsellors, teachers, year advisers, careers advisers, the principal and senior teachers are available to assist students and their families. All work to create safe, caring schools, free from violence and discrimination. All can help you or your child in different ways. School counsellors are experienced teachers who have a degree in psychology and post-graduate qualifications in school counselling. They work with students of all ages, and their families, from pre-school to year 12. Their work is varies, with attention focused on developmental stages of student growth, including the needs, tasks, and student interests related to those stages.

Professional school counsellors implement a comprehensive school counselling programme that promotes and enhances student achievement. They provide counselling programmes in three domains: academic, career and personal/social. Their services and programs help students resolve emotional, social or behavioural problems and help them develop a clearer focus or sense of direction. Effective counselling programs are important to the school climate and a crucial element in improving student achievement.

This comprehensive, practical and research-based resource offers step-by-step guidance to assist school counsellor in working on a wide variety of pre-teen and adolescent issues. It considers the various theories of counselling and issues of counselling in school settings and focuses on the development of school counselling skills including basic interviewing and other assessment skills, with an emphasis on therapeutic listening skills. Emphasis is placed upon the acquisition of skills related to empathy, the counsellor-student relationship, and the establishment of a therapeutic alliance in the context of cultural diversity.

Dr. Ramesh Chaturvedi

Contents

1

Elementary School Counselling

The elementary school counselling and guidance programme is a part of the total school programme and complements learning in the classroom. It is child-centered, preventive, and developmental. The programme encourages students' social, emotional, and personal growth at each stage of their development.

The purpose of counselling with students, parents, and teachers is to help students maximise their potential. The elementary school counsellor also conducts guidance lessons; consults with parents, teachers, and other professionals; and coordinates student services in the school. This counselling and guidance programme provides elementary students with assistance in:

– Understanding self and developing a positive self-image.
– Showing respect for the feelings of others.
– Understanding the decision-making process.
– Maintaining effective relationships with peers and adults.
– Developing effective study skills.

- Being prepared to make the transition to the intermediate school.
- Gaining an understanding of the world of work.

Qualification of Elementary School Guidance Counsellor

1. A master's degree
2. Special preparation in the following areas:
   - child growth and development
   - individual counselling skills
   - group counselling and guidance skills
   - communication skills
   - elements of career development
   - educational and psychological measurement
   - theory and practice of counselling including exceptional and culturally diverse children
   - philosophy and principles of guidance
   - research and evaluation
   - elementary school guidance

Counselling is conducted with students and parents individually and in small groups when requested and determined appropriate. It is short-term, voluntary, and confidential. Parental permission is obtained prior to any extended individual or group counselling. Students are seen by the counsellor when:

- Parents request and indicate a need and desire that the counsellor meet with their children.

- Students request counselling.
- Teachers, administrators, or other school staff refer the student.

Parents are informed of counselling groups for children and adults. Groups counselling sessions for children focus on building self-esteem, learning how to make or keep friends, developing good study habits, improving communication skills, preparing for the intermediate school, and coping with changing family situations. Topics for parent groups include child-rearing concerns, child development, and methods parents may use to help children experience healthy development and success in school.

Benefits of Counselling

The elementary school counsellor works directly with students in individual and group counselling sessions as well as in classroom guidance lessons so students may:

- Be successful in school.
- Establish effective study skills.
- Adjust to a new school.
- Develop positive feelings about work, family, and society.
- Build positive feelings towards self and others.
- Develop skills in interacting and communicating with others.
- Cope with change in themselves and their surroundings.
- Identify and accept their own and others' strengths and weaknesses.

– Recognise the causes and effects of their actions.

– Become responsible for their own behaviour.

– Receive crisis intervention when necessary.

The guidance counsellor helps students become motivated learners and encourages them to discuss concerns with their parents. When students work through their social and emotional issues, with the help of their parents and the counsellor, they are able to devote attention and energy to the intellectual tasks at school.

The elementary school guidance counsellor works with parents through individual consultation, joint consultation with the children's teachers, and parent discussion groups. In these ways the counsellor assists parents to:

– Understand their children's progress in school.

– Select strategies to motivate their children.

– Develop realistic goals with their children.

– Become actively involved in their children's school life.

– Understand the educational programme K-12.

The counsellor may lead parent education and discussion groups and serve as a resource when parents study or discuss child-related issues. The counsellor consults with parents to identify students with special abilities and/or needs. In this capacity the counsellor helps parents understand the services available from other school staff such as the school psychologist, social worker, and resource teachers. The counsellor helps parents find other professionals within the school system or within the larger community when extra support is needed.

The elementary school guidance counsellor is an integral part of the total elementary school programme. The counsellor observes children; consults with teachers, psychologists, and social workers; gathers and provides resources; conducts classroom guidance lessons; collaborates on classroom intervention; conducts joint parent conferences; reviews and interprets school records; and serves on committees that plan for the individual needs of specific children. The elementary school guidance counsellor helps teachers by:

- Consulting with them concerning children.
- Planning small group and classroom activities to meet specific needs of students.
- Gathering and sharing resources.
- Observing children in the classroom or on the playground.
- Conferencing with parents.
- Reviewing student records and discussing their implications with the teachers and/or parents.
- Coordinating staff efforts to work with individual students.
- Promoting a positive school climate.
- Explaining the academic programme K-12.

The elementary school counsellor is a vital resource for the school staff. He or she coordinates and helps implement the staff's efforts to meet the needs of students individually, in small groups of students, and in entire classrooms.

The entire community benefits from the elementary school counselling and guidance programme because:

- All students in the entire school system are served.

– A clearly defined curriculum provides information about the programme to the community.
– Business, industry, and labour can participate actively in the programme.
– A potential work force is provided with decision-making skills and preemployment skills.

Multicultural Education in Elementary and Secondary Schools.

The introduction of multicultural activities has been motivated by at least four intentions:

(1) to remedy ethnocentrism in the traditional curriculum;

(2) to build understanding among racial and cultural groups and appreciation of different cultures;

(3) to defuse intergroup tensions and conflicts; and

(4) to make the curricula relevant to the experiences, cultural traditions, and historical contributions of the nation's diverse population.

Many educators now assert that a growing body of evidence links multicultural education and improved academic learning. For example, Hale described cognitive gains achieved by children in a pre-school programme integrating material on African American culture throughout the curriculum. Zaslavsky demonstrated how elements of African and other cultural traditions can be used to teach complex mathematics concepts to inner-city students. A study using three elementary programmes for Hispanic children not English-proficient revealed that the math, reading, and language scores of students in bilingual and multiculturally-integrated English as a Second Language programmes were significantly superior to scores of students enrolled in bilingual ESL without the multicultural integration.

Hylton and Dumett present a list of suggestions for elementary level class activities focusing on multicultural themes:

- collect articles from newspapers and magazines that deal with one or more groups.
- collect relevant pictures, books, records, and poems.
- perform plays about various groups.
- keep a journal based on one or more themes, such as money around the world, or holidays around the world.
- develop a multicultural calendar.
- learn songs in different languages.
- make maps showing the origin of various groups.

An example of a more comprehensive multicultural programme is Project REACH (Respecting Ethnic and Cultural Heritage), which has gained prominence as an academic discipline-based programme for middle school social studies, and which now includes over 60,000 students and hundreds of teachers in twelve states. REACH infuses information on the history and culture of various groups into the regular curriculum. It is a multicultural curriculum and process, and teacher training process, managed on a school- or district-wide basis, organised around four phases:

- Human Relations Skills. Students participate in activities on self-awareness, self-esteem, interpersonal communication, and understanding group dynamics.

- Cultural Self Awareness. Students conduct research on their personal culture, family history, or community.
- Multicultural Awareness. Students study from booklets on American history from diverse ethnic points of view.
- Cross Cultural Experience. Historical and cultural information in the booklets is made personal through dialogue and exchange with students and adults from different ethnic groups.

According to Jones, multicultural learning activities are most effective for learners when they:

- offer students opportunities to observe/participate in the affairs of the community.
- engage students directly and actively in learning.
- relate directly to the concerns of the students.
- rely on a broad range of instructional materials.
- offer a scope and sequence that is developmentally based.
- evaluate and document what has been learned using tests, demonstrations, surveys and other assessment methods.

The Portland Public Schools provides an example of a multicultural education programme that has been implemented as a result of a community-wide mandate. The impetus for change came from the creation of a district desegregation plan, and a coalition of civic and church organisations stimulated public dialogue on the goals for multicultural education. Information was conveyed to the public in various fors such as publications, forums, and teach-ins. Ultimately, a series of essays on cultural contributions of African Americans, Native Americans, Asians, and Hispanic Americans became the basis of the curriculum used throughout the district.

Interdisciplinary Programmes

Needs Assessment. Decisions must be made regarding the grade(s) to be involved, the availability of materials and the development of others, hiring of new teachers, and training of current teachers.

Goals. Besides the district- or state-mandated student performance goals, goals for skills development and attitude change should be specified for each subject area and grade.

Curriculum Development. Most multicultural materials currently available are concentrated in the field of social studies. Two key issues to be addressed in the development of materials for other courses are the extent to which they reinforce student competency goals and the degree of their integration into the school's formal instructional programme.

Multicultural materials have been developed by organisations and commercial publishers to support individual class lessons, as part of a course unit, to develop school-wide activities, or as the basis for an entire curriculum in one or more subject areas. Some of these materials can be identified by writing to the addresses below or with assistance from a librarian or other information specialist. Staff Development. Barron and others identify a set of considerations to overcome potential problems and obstacles:

- View multicultural education as a process, and as an integral part of the school.

- Specify outcomes; link goals for multicultural education to district or school goals for student learning.
- Center efforts around students, not teachers. Advisory committees should include parents and educators but should consist mostly of students. At the same time, respect the right of teachers to make professional choices for effectively meeting learning objectives.

The role of programme coordinator should be a paid position. If the programme coordinator is responsible for other duties (teaching, guidance/counselling), he or she should be provided with release time. In addition, successful programmes require a commitment from leadership, which might consist of the department chair, school principal, or district superintendent. Plans for school- or district-wide multicultural education programmes should be comprehensive, focused and well-publicised. Plans should also be long-term with measurable goals, staged timelines, resources and accountabilities. Burton examines the issue of student resistance to learning about other cultures and cautions consideration of two groups of students: those in the group the class is celebrating and who will be sensitive about the observance, and those not in the group who may not be interested and may be prejudiced against the celebrated group.

2

School Counsellor Performance

Assessment is the most controversial area within counsellor education. Knowledge needed by counsellors to obtain evidence, evaluate its usefulness, and interpret its meaning have long been and continue to be debated. An efficient, but fair assessment of counsellor performance focuses primarily on what the counsellor actually does—not on counsellor skills, training or experience, and not on student outcomes.

Assessment of prerequisite counsellor skills wastes time and effort in that it duplicates other forms of evaluation. Attempting to link student outcomes exclusively to individual counsellor performance is unfair in that many factors other than counselling influence student learning and behaviour. While accountability for student outcomes is important, it belongs to a broader programme evaluation which takes these other factors into account.

Counsellor assessment criteria must be based on clear role priorities in the current job setting—for example, developmental/preventative vs. crisis/remedial activities, counselling students vs. counselling with parents or teachers, academic/career vs. personal/social counselling, and counselling vs. administrative/clerical tasks. Once these priorities have been clarified, administrators and counsellors should define realistic expectations of time to be spent and tasks to be accomplished. This collaboration could result in guidelines for an assessment instrument which could be used by counsellors to monitor their own priorities and time.

In most counsellor performance assessments, programme administrators will want to know not only what the counsellor does, but how well he/she does it. Is accurate information given to students? Are school policies observed by the counsellor? Are tasks performed efficiently? These types of assessments often require subjective judgments which may be threatening to counsellors. Identifying very specific examples of each desired behaviour can reduce subjectivity, and obtaining counsellor input about the validity of these descriptions can reduce counsellor anxiety.

The most critical measurement issue in performance assessment is validity. Is specific "job-relatedness" built into the assessment instrument? Does it actually measure what it says it measures? There is no one instrument, either in format or in content, that can be used universally to assess school counsellor performance. To be valid in a particular setting, the instrument must reflect the priorities of the school, the district, or the state conducting the assessment. Constructing a useful counsellor performance assessment instrument does not require extensive measurement expertise.

Once the relevant participants in the assessment process agree on the job-relatedness of the tasks and behaviours to be assessed, a simple and easy-to-use instrument may be developed. The goal is to produce a tool that will actually be used, not a sophisticated measurement device for collecting research data. The form may be a simple one-page checklist, in which each item represents one major objective, or a several-page document, in which each objective is broken into specific tasks or characteristic behaviours. Similarly, the response called for by each item may be a check mark indicating the presence of a characteristic or completion of a task or a numerical rating with each number representing a specific behaviour description. Vague, low-to-high options should be avoided.

Even if the form is to be used primarily for assessing minimal competency or "adequate" job performance, it should contain item response options that address the full range of evaluation from unsatisfactory to outstanding and/ or highly creative performance. This expands the potential usefulness of the assessment process as a positive strategy for facilitating ongoing counsellor growth and development.

In the 1960's, tests were viewed positively and were used primarily to identify students of outstanding abilities. However, in the early 1970's, Goldman suggested, using a well-known metaphor, that the marriage between tests and counselling had failed. At about that time, courts prohibited some established tests for certain purposes and legislatures passed bills to regulate aspects of the use of standardised tests.

The validity and practical utility of all testing and appraisal techniques were questioned and negative consequences of "labelling" were emphasised. Yet assessment remained commonplace in schools. Consider these findings in a survey by Engen, Lamb, and Prediger and reported by Zytowski: 93% of secondary schools administered at least one test to all students; 76% administered achievement test batteries; 66% administered academic aptitude or intelligent tests; and 16% administered inventories of school or social adjustment or personality tests. By the 1980's, vocational guidance, according to Zytowski, had become a unifying force between counselling and testing.

Zytowski described several changes that had been made in tests, themselves, and in their uses in counselling. One of these was an erosion of reliance on predictive validity and an accompanying emphasis on convergent and discriminant validity, along with construct validity. He also described the value of an assessment in terms of its ability to guide and motivate a professional toward seeking additional information for decision making.

De-formalising assessment, another change, included increased use of one-item measures, informed self estimates, and card sorts or inventories in which quantified outcomes are less important than is the process the client engages in. Computers had become more instrumental in testing, from primarily scoring and score reporting to actual test administration and providing immediate feedback. Availability and interest in computer testing have clearly increased in the decade since Zytowski's summary appeared. The counselling community has become more aware of ethical issues in testing.

An American Counselling Association (ACA) statement titled Responsibilities of Users of Standardised Tests (RUST), published in 1978 and revised in 1989, urges awareness of differing purposes for testing and reminds us to consider the limitations of tests for any purpose and to evaluate the costs of not testing or using alternative methods of gathering the information needed.

Assessment Skills

The roles that have been identified imply that counsellors should have certain skills related to assessment. Schafer and Mufson organised these into three areas: doing pupil assessment, doing programme evaluation, and using basic research. Doing pupil assessment includes: types of assessment; assessment systems and programmes; test administration and scoring; test reporting and interpretation; test evaluation and selection; design, analysis, and improvement in instrument development; formal and informal methods of assessment; methods for using assessment in counselling; administrative uses of assessment; computer-based applications; and ethics of using assessments.

Doing programme evaluation includes: needs assessment; formative and summative evaluation; sources of evaluation research invalidity (instrumental, internal, and external); choosing evaluation designs; choices of and computational methods for descriptive and inferential statistics; writing evaluation proposals and reports; disseminating information; and research ethics. Using basic research includes: locating and obtaining relevant research reports; reading and summarising research reports; evaluating validity of instruments and research designs; and purpose and assumptions of common inferential statistical procedures.

Test Interpretation Skills

School counsellors are often asked to administer and interpret norm-referenced tests. Certain fundamental test interpretation skills are necessary to accurately interpret and utilise test data.

Norm-referenced Tests

Norm-referenced tests are assessments administered to students to determine how they perform in comparison to others. They are often used to classify students for placement and award purposes. A student's current test performance is compared to that of a representative sample of students, known as a norm group, who were previously administered the test. Norm groups can be used to create either national norms or local norms, depending on who is included in the normative sample.

Norm-referenced tests have several strengths. For example, Dombrowski points out that norm-referenced testing often allows for reliable and objective measurement. However, with these types of assessments, it is critical to understand the composition of the norm group. It's also important to note that test scores on norm-referenced tests typically rise the longer the test is in use, likely due to changes in instruction or test preparation that are made as educators become more familiar with the form of a test.

Criterion-referenced and norm-referenced tests yield different, but complementary, pieces of information. Criterion-referenced tests, such as many of the state high school tests, help demonstrate how a student stands in relation to a given educational curriculum. The emphasis is not on comparison with other students, but rather, on mastery of specific content knowledge and skills. Criterion-referenced tests provide useful information about students' strengths and weaknesses in various curriculum areas. It is critical that the content domain of the assessment be clearly defined. Results of norm- and criterion-referenced tests should be combined with other formal and informal data collection methods, since no single set of test scores is adequate to make important educational decisions.

Properties of the Normal Curve

In norm-referenced tests, a child's test performance is compared to a norm group. The distribution of test scores generated by the norm group is normal. Therefore, understanding what a normal curve is becomes critical for norm-referenced test interpretation. First, a school counsellor should recognise that if he or she were to draw a vertical line down the center of the normal curve, the distribution would be divided into two equal halves. Because both halves are identical, statisticians classify normal curves as symmetrical.

The vertical line represents the mean, or average, performance of the norm group. With normal curves, this line also represents the median and the mode; however, this is not always true of other types of curves. Knowing the mean helps the test interpreter to identify the average performance of the norm group, but is not sufficient to correctly interpret an individual's performance on a norm-referenced test. The school counsellor also must know how the concept of standard deviation is related to the normal curve. Drummond indicates that standard deviation is a statistic that defines the spread of scores around the mean. Standard deviation helps determine how far above or below the norm group mean an individual's score falls.

For practical purposes, the normal curve is divided into three standard deviations above the mean and three standard deviations below the mean. In a normal curve, 34% of individuals fall between the mean and one standard deviation above the mean, 14% of individuals fall between one standard deviation above the mean and two standard deviations above the mean, and 2% of individual fall between two standard deviations above the mean and three standard deviations above the mean. Since the normal curve is symmetrical, the percentages are the same for the standard deviations above and below the mean.

Properties of Common Score Types

To accurately and efficiently interpret norm-referenced assessments, school counsellors need to be familiar with the properties of common scores they may encounter. Those score types are Z scores, T scores, NCE scores, and stanine scores.

- Z scores have a fixed mean of 0 and a standard deviation of 1. Thus, if a student's test performance is one standard deviation above the mean, the individual has a Z score of 1. If a student's test score is two standard deviations below the mean, his or her Z score is a -2. It is possible (and common) for students to have negative Z scores.
- T scores often have a mean of 50 and a standard deviation of 10. Thus, if a student's test performance is one standard deviation below the mean, the individual has a T score of 40. If a student's test score is at the mean, his or her T score is 50.
- NCE scores stands for normal curve equivalent scores. NCE scores have a fixed mean of 50 and a standard deviation of approximately 21. If a student's test performance is two standard deviations above the mean, the individual has an NCE score of 92. If a student's test score is one standard deviation below the mean, his or her NCE score is a 29.
- Stanine scores have a fixed mean of 5 and a standard deviation of 2. The term "stanine" stands for Standard Nine, indicating that the range of stanine scores is fixed from 1 to 9, with 9 representing the highest possible stanine score, and 1 representing the possible score. If a student's test performance is two standard deviations above the mean, the individual has a stanine score of 9. If a student's test score is three standard deviations

below the mean, his or her stanine score is a 1. Five is the most commonly assigned stanine score, because it falls directly on the mean the curve. If a student is assigned a 5, he or she is performing better than half of the norm group on the content assessed on the norm-referenced test.

Difference between Percent and Percentile

School counsellors need to recognise that percent and percentile are different concepts. The term "percent" is an abbreviation of the Latin phrase per centum, which literally means "by the hundred." A percent represents the proportion of test material answered correctly out of a hundred. For example, if an individual took a 50-item test and answered 25 items correctly, the percent he or she got correct would be 50.

Percentiles, according to Drummond, are one of most common tools to help interpret norm-referenced assessments. Percentile scores range from 1 to 99 and tell the test interpreter the percentage of individuals in the norm-group that the test taker outperformed. For example, if a test taker earned a score in the 74th percentile, the interpretation would be that 74% of the norm group performed at or below the test taker's score.

Ability of Translating One Standard Score to Another

Once school counsellors have developed competency with the four skills addressed above, they will have the tools necessary to quickly and accurately translate scores from one common score type to another. This skill is particularly important when meeting with parents and students to discuss their norm-referenced test performance. School counsellors need to be cognisant that parents and students are often confused by the many different score types, the compact layout of many norm-reference score reporting sheets, and most importantly, the interpretation of the scores. This is an opportunity for the informed school counsellor to be particularly helpful. Because the score types discussed above (Z, T, NCE, stanine) are all based on the properties of the normal curve, the scores can easily be converted from one score type to another.

By performing test score conversions, the school counsellor can demonstrate to the parent(s) and student how the different score types are representative of how the test taker performed in comparison with the norm group. For example, if a student had a Z score of 1, the individual's performance is one standard deviation above the mean. Eighty-four percent of the norm group performed at or below the test taker's score. The student also had a T score of 60, an NCE score of 71, and a stanine score of 7.

All of the scores are one standard deviation above the mean. The same is true for students who have scores that fall below the mean. If a student's norm-referenced test score is two standard deviations below the mean, the corresponding Z score is -2, the T score is 30, the NCE score is 8, and the stanine is 1. Due to the increased reliance on norm-referenced tests in schools, it is essential that school counsellors be able to accurately interpret and explain test results to various stakeholders. While these five test interpretation skills do not guarantee expertise, they are intended to encourage school counsellors' minimum competency with regard to norm-referenced test interpretation.

Assessing Student Engagement Rates

Early studies of student engagement often focused on time-on-task behaviours. Student engagement has been used to depict students' willingness to participate in routine school activities, such as attending classes, submitting required work, and following teachers' directions in class.

The opposite of engagement is disaffection. Disaffected children are passive, do not tryhard, and give up easily in the face of challenges [they can] be bored, depressed, anxious, or even angry about their presence in the classroom; they can be withdrawn from learning opportunities or even rebellious towards teachers and classmates. From a different perspective, Pintrich and & De Groot associated engagement levels with students' use of cognitive, meta-cognitive and self-regulatory strategies to monitor and guide their learning processes.

In this view, student engagement is viewed as motivated behaviour apparent from the kinds of cognitive strategies students choose to use (e.g., simple or "surface" processing strategies such as rehearsal versus "deeper" processing strategies such as elaboration), and by their willingness to persist with difficult tasks by regulating their own learning behaviour. Use of cognitive and meta-cognitive strategies may be taken to indicate active task engagement, while use of shallow strategies may be taken to indicate superficial engagement.

Methods for Measuring Engagement

The most common way that student engagement is measured is through information reported by the students themselves. Other methods include checklists and rating scales completed by teachers, observations, work sample analyses, and case studies. Each of these methods is described briefly below.

Self-Reports: Students may be asked to complete surveys or questionnaires regarding their level of task engagement. Items relating to the cognitive aspects of engagement often ask students to report on factors such as their attention versus distraction during class, the mental effort they expend on these tasks (e.g., to integrate new concepts with previous knowledge), and task persistence (e.g., their reaction to perceived failure to comprehend the course material). Students can also be asked to report on their response levels during class time (e.g., making verbal responses within group discussions, looking for distractions, and engaging in non-academic social interaction) as an index of behavioural task engagement.

Affective engagement questions typically ask students to rate their interest in and emotional reactions to learning tasks on indices such as choice of activities (e.g., selection of more versus less challenging tasks), the desire to know more about particular topics, and feelings of stimulation or excitement in beginning new projects. In addition to asking the question of whether students are engaged in learning tasks, self-report measures can provide some indication of why this is the case.

Research into achievement goal orientations, for example, has indicated positive relationships between task or mastery goals, which reflect a desire for knowledge or skill acquisition, and students' use of effective learning strategies. Studies have also demonstrated positive relationships between students' perceived learning control and adaptive learning processes.

Checklists and Rating Scales: In addition to student self-report measures, a few studies have used summative rating scales to measure student engagement levels. For example, the teacher report scales used by Skinner & Belmont asked teachers to assess their students' willingness to participate in school tasks (i.e., effort, attention, and persistence during the initiation and execution of learning activities, such as "When faced with a difficult problem, this student doesn't try"), as well as their emotional reactions to these tasks (i.e., interest versus boredom, happiness versus sadness, anxiety and anger, such as "When in class, this student seems happy").

The Teacher Questionnaire on Student Motivation to Read developed by Sweet, Guthrie, & Ng asks teachers to report on factors relating to student engagement rates, such as activities (e.g., enjoys reading about favourite activities), autonomy (e.g., knows how to choose a book he or she would want to read), and individual factors (e.g., is easily distracted while reading).

Direct Observations: Although self-report scales are widely used, the validity of the data yielded by these measures will vary considerably with students' abilities to accurately assess their own cognitions, behaviours, and affective responses. Direct observations are often used to confirm students' reported levels of engagement in learning tasks. A number of established protocols are available in this area. Most of these observational studies have used some form of momentary time sampling system. In these methods, the observer records whether a behaviour was present or absent at the moment that the time interval ends or else during a specific time period.

In classwide observations, approximately 5 minutes of observational data can generally be collected on each target student per lesson. Thus, a 30-minute observation period would allow observations of approximately 5 target students, with 6 to 7 sessions being required to observe a full class. In addition, to obtain a representative sample of students' behaviour over the full course of a lesson, observations are generally rotated across students so that each student is observed continuously for only one minute at a time.

Work Sample Analyses: Evidence of higher-order problem-solving and metacognitive learning strategies can be gathered from sources such as student projects, portfolios, performances, exhibitions, and learning journals or logs. The efficacy of these methods hinges on the use of suitably structured tasks and scoring rubrics. For example, a rubric to assess the application of higher-order thinking skills in a student portfolio might include criteria for evidence of problem-solving, planning, and self-evaluation in the work.

A number of formal and informal protocols for assessing students' self-regulated learning strategies also incorporate components that focus on metacognitive skills. The Metacognitive Knowledge Monitoring Assessment and the Assessment of Cognitive Monitoring Effectiveness are more targeted measures suitable for use in classroom situations and with demonstrated sound psychometric properties in empirical evaluations.

Focused Case Studies: When the focus of an investigation is restricted to a small group of target students, it is often more useful to collect detailed descriptive accounts of engagement rates. Case studies allow researchers to address questions of student engagement inductively by recording details about students in interaction with other people and objects within classrooms. These accounts should describe both students' behaviours and the classroom contexts in which they occur. This might include, for example, the behaviour of peers, direct antecedents to the target student's behaviours (e.g., teacher directions), as well as the student's response and the observed consequences of that response.

Case studies generally attempt to place observations of engagement within the total context of the classroom and/ or school, and are concerned as much with the processes associated with engagement as they are in depicting engagement levels. Teachers interested in assessing student engagement in the classroom should consider using separate measures to get at the cognitive, affective, and behavioural aspects of task engagement. Within each of these domain areas, using a range of methods can also strengthen the validity of findings and provide alternative perspectives on the results. Teachers may wish to include measures that address the question of why students do, or do not, engage with particular types of tasks.

Planning and Integrating Basic Skills

Postsecondary students are not graduating with the "basic skills" needed for success at work, at home, and in further education. What are these basic skills? The contemporary list goes far beyond the traditional Three R's to include the attitudes, knowledge, and behaviours needed to function in an increasingly self directed, interpersonal, and technological workplace. In addition to reading, writing, and computing, these skills include:

- learning to learn;
- effective verbal and nonverbal communication;
- adaptability (including creative thinking and problem solving);
- personal management (including self esteem, goal setting/motivation, and personal/career development);

– group effectiveness (including personal skills, negotiation, and teamwork);
– influence (including organisational effectiveness and leadership);
– the ability to understand technology;
– the ability to apply scientific knowledge to work situations; and
– the ability to balance and manage family and work.

Schools are being challenged to integrate these new basic skills across their curricula. This presents school counsellors with an opportunity: if they can prove their effectiveness in helping students plan for and acquire the basic skills and prepare for life after high school, they can trade their traditionally services oriented, possibly expendable positions in schools for positions of influence in matters such as school reform and restructuring.

Currently, the most promising models for helping school counsellors take this active role are "comprehensive counselling and guidance programmes." Comprehensive counselling and guidance programmes are the "umbrella programmes" of the 1990s, designed to provide all students with life competencies through personal, social, and career counselling. Abandoning the traditionally passive, service approach to counselling, comprehensive counselling and guidance programmes employ four interactive components that take the vagueness out of the school counsellor's role:

1. *The Guidance Curriculum*: counsellors provide structured, competency based activities in the classroom or in group situations, using this focused time with students to focus on content areas such as self knowledge, educational and occupational exploration, and career planning.

2. *Individual Planning*: Counsellors help students think ahead and think for themselves, teaching them how to plan rigorous and coherent sequences of courses, as well as monitor and manage their lives.

3. *Responsive Services*: Counsellors meet the immediate needs of students confronting personal or educational challenges.

4. *System Support*: Counsellors work to sustain and enhance the implementation of comprehensive counselling and guidance programmes.

An essential part of the effort to equip students with the basic skills is the integration of academic and vocational instruction. Basic competencies in these areas are prerequisites for lifetime learning. Additionally, as technology continues to become more sophisticated, the competencies with which students graduate are rapidly becoming requirements for landing and keeping good jobs with growth potential. Conversely, college-bound students can benefit from vocational methods of instruction and experiences connecting school to work. By using academic theory in real life settings, they can acquire skills needed outside the classroom.

Schools emphasising acquisition of the basic skills recognise the critical role counsellors can play in helping students plan a demanding sequence of academic and vocational courses that will prepare them both for employment and postsecondary education. School counsellors promote the idea that vocational education is better supported when vocational and academic education are seen as complementary strategies for student success, not as competing programmes of study. An example: a Pittsburgh, Pennsylvania, school district has discontinued its general education track. Students must now make specific curriculum choices early on. It is therefore necessary for guidance professionals to contact all students earlier and stay in contact with them.

To receive a diploma, each student must plan and complete a focused curriculum leading to an academic or an applied technology and career development certificate, or both. To inform the community about the methods the district is using to infuse career education into curriculum, the district sends letters to parents of all eighth graders, and requires all tenth graders to view a video explaining graduation and certificate requirements within a group guidance class. Counsellors now find it much easier to promote the merits of Pittsburgh's 40 vocational options and their relation to graduation, the workplace, and postsecondary education. This action, along with other initiatives, has significantly reduced dropout rates.

Without a comprehensive counselling and guidance programme to address the needs of all students, developmental needs are overlooked and students unable to state their needs fall through the cracks. Due to the large student to counsellor ratios, many students end up selecting courses based on availability, instructor popularity, or other criteria that may have nothing to do with career plans, learning styles or basic skill needs. Traditionally, counsellors have been rewarded for attending to students who already know their career needs and their principal's priorities. Little attention has been given to what has been called the "forgotten half".

Part of this stems from the nebulous role of school counsellors. Counsellors are expected to perform roles as varied as the schools within which they work. Some are advocates for students confronting severe family and social change, while others are saddled with large amounts of "administrivia." Many confront substance abuse, suicide, and teen pregnancy as regular parts of their day. Comprehensive counselling and guidance programmes call for counsellors' reduced involvement in administrative and clerical work. They place counsellors in fewer one-on-one counselling situations. At the same time, they strengthen counsellors' accountability for effectively helping all students prepare for the world beyond high school.

Unfortunately, implementing comprehensive counselling and guidance programmes has been a low priority in the school reform movement. This could be due to

(a) hesitancy of school counsellors to vocalise their positions,

(b) school counsellors' traditional isolation from schools' mainstream instructional programmes, or

(c) school counsellors' limited involvement in reform.

Implementing comprehensive counselling and guidance programmes on a large scale requires the revamping and greater standardisation of school counsellors' education. Preservice school counsellors need a more specific, focused programme that arms them with the essentials of professional renewal. School counsellor education should be built on a foundation of educational developmental theory and practice as well as psychological theory. Preservice school counsellors need training in several areas:

1) helping students plan their coursework and futures;

2) promoting curricula and instructional methods which integrate academic and vocational education; and

3) implementing comprehensive counselling and guidance programmes.

Performance Assessment

It is important to be open and specific about the purpose of a performance assessment. Counsellors should know if it will be used to determine promotions or pay increases, to provide constructive feedback for professional development, or simply to meet administrative requirements. They also should know what instrument will be used, who will conduct the assessment, when it will be conducted, and when they will be informed of the results. Conducting the assessment collaboratively, with counsellors and assessors responding to and discussing each item, is highly recommended.

Performance assessment can be time-consuming for both the assessor and assessee; to be cost-effective, it should serve as many people in as many ways as possible. Viewed positively and constructively, a performance assessment can go well beyond a pro forma documentation of minimal competency. It can address new and emerging areas of professional expertise and can serve as a challenge to maximise the ongoing professional development of even the most competent and experienced counsellor.

Supervision of School Counsellors

Professionally appropriate supervision is emerging as a highly effective means of nurturing school counsellors' professional development. New challenges in schools and increased understanding of the complexity of professional development dictate the need for increased attention to and use of effective supervision practices. Today's children and youth need highly skilled help in managing the complicated situations in which they live. School counsellors see an increasing number of suicidal children as well as adolescents.

The upsurge in substance abuse, gang involvement, and violence are well publicised. Increasingly, parents turn to the schools to help them solve problems that face them, including those posed by their children. In order to effectively help children in their classrooms, teachers seek consultative help from counsellors. The comprehensive guidance programmes being implemented in today's schools call for school counsellors to use all of their professional skills. Focused and constructive supervision is of benefit to all practitioners whether they are novices or experienced, highly competent or insufficiently trained. Due to reductions in caseloads, renewed commitment to elementary counselling, and retirement of counsellors who entered the field in the 1960's, the number of new school counsellors is increasing.

Although it is a relatively new discipline, supervision is compatibly defined in both education and in counselling. The purpose of supervision is the growth and enhanced effectiveness of the practitioner. "It is characterised by a cycle of feedback, practice, and additional feedback", based on interpretation of gathered data in light of established standards. Because of the emphasis on skill-based performance evaluations generated by educational reform, many states have defined school counsellors' roles and needed competencies: programme management, counselling, guidance, consulting, coordinating, student appraisal, and referral. With these behavioural standards as a basis, supervisors and counsellors operate with the same definitions for effective performance. The value of timely feedback has been reinforced in the career-ladder-related-teacher-appraisal systems, setting the climate for the same practice for all categories of educators.

Clinical, Developmental and Administrative Supervision

When competently done, supervision not only enhances the quality of counsellors' skills, but also helps hone professional judgment, "encourages greater self-awareness, and fosters an integrated professional and personal identity as a counsellor". Barret and Schmidt outlined a useful schema for distinguishing between the kinds of supervision needed for/by school counsellors: clinical, developmental, and administrative. In this distinction, the purpose of each supervision type accounts for the different procedures used by the various supervisors available in schools. The purpose of clinical supervision is enhancement of counsellors' professional skills and ethical functioning.

The data sources which support clinical supervision include observations of counsellors applying their professional skills and values. In the school setting, the typical opportunities for gathering data to support clinical supervision are available (e.g., live and/or recorded observations, case presentations, and consultations). Clinical supervisors must be counsellors who are competent in the school counsellor functions and in supervision practices. The purpose of developmental supervision is improvement of the guidance and counselling programme and counsellors' pursuit of professional development.

Data sources which support developmental supervision are recordings of goals and activities undertaken to attain goals and measures of goal attainment, programme plans and implementation calendars, self-reports, and consumer satisfaction surveys. Developmental supervision is best provided by competent school counsellors from the same system as the supervisee. The purpose of administrative supervision is assurance that counsellors have worthy work habits, comply with laws and policies, relate well with other school staff and parents, and otherwise work effectively within the school system.

Data sources supporting administrative supervision are such things as work schedules, recordkeeping and documentation systems, and evidence of team efforts. Either school counsellor supervisors or building administrators may be providers of administrative supervision.

Particularly relevant in the school setting is clarifying the place of supervision in the overall system for helping counsellors' improve their performance. Whether or how data used in supervision will apply to summative evaluation needs to be spelled out. Supervision provides opportunities for personalising the professional development processes. The combination of feedback from supervision and from performance appraisal is data which counsellors and their supervisors use as the basis for professional development goals.

The cyclical nature of the supervisory process is enhanced by the lengthy supervisor-supervisee relationships typical of elementary and secondary school settings. The multiple opportunities for supervision over significant lengths of time allow supervisory relationships to be rich ones. The primary obstacles to fully effective school counsellor supervision are caused by the insufficient number of school counsellor-competent supervisors.

Where there are such supervisors, there is little or no relevant counsellor-supervisor training available and/or no specialised certification required. Although the building principals can provide useful administrative supervision, it is unlikely that they are current in the clinical functions of counselling. Competent school counsellors are usually available to fulfil the developmental and clinical supervision roles, but they often lack training and certification in supervision. Although development of the appropriate job descriptions and provision of the relevant training at this time are the responsibility of local school districts, the Standards for Counselling Supervisors and the Curriculum Guide provide the guidelines needed.

A pool of potential clinical and/or developmental supervisors are available in many communities. Current school counsellors can fulfil roles as peer supervisors. An increasing number of mid-sized school systems employ central office-based guidance supervisors. Some intermediate education agencies and some state departments of education provide such expertise. Schools are also contracting with community-based, Licensed Professional Counsellors, or counsellor educators.

Supervision of professional practice is an effective, but perhaps underutilised means of nurturing the professional development of new and experienced school counsellors. It is a personalised vehicle for assuring that children, their families, and teachers benefit from quality services. For counsellor supervision to be practiced more universally in the nation's schools, states need to require appropriate certification, counsellor education programmes need to offer appropriate counselling supervisor training, and schools and district counselling supervisors need to report their counsellor supervision practices and findings.

Job Role Expectations of School Counsellors

In their study of skills needed by school counsellors, Schafer and Mufson reviewed job analyses conducted by five school districts in five different states. They found a natural division of the job role expectations of school counsellors into six areas: counselling (individual and group), pupil assessment, consultation, information officer, school programme facilitator, and research and evaluation. There are assessment-intensive aspects of each of these.

The counsellor's major function in the school is to counsel students individually and whenever practical in small or large groups. The counsellor also is responsible for identifying students with special needs. These activities include interpreting test scores and non-test data.

Pupil assessment includes scheduling and preparing for testing, scoring them or sending them out for scoring, recording results, and scheduling for interpretation. Counsellors are also responsible for assisting students in evaluating their aptitudes and abilities through interpreting standardised tests. They may be expected to advise teachers who need to understand psychological evaluations and who are interested in improving their content-referenced testing skills.

The third function is that of a consultant. The counsellor consults with and advises teachers, parents, and administrators in guidance matters and test score interpretation. In some schools the counsellor helps teachers with psychological evaluations and content-referenced testing and advises school committees in selection of tests.

The function of information officer includes informing parents, teachers, and staff about counselling services, informing employers and colleges about students according to school policy, and ensuring two-way communication between school and home. Many of these activities involve test interpretation.

The fifth function is administrative, including school administration and counselling administration. Within school administration, the counsellor is responsible for administering tests. Within counselling administrative functions, the counsellor is expected to analyse guidance services. Also, the counsellor is often asked to participate in decisions about the instructional curriculum.

The sixth function is research and evaluation. The counsellor may be responsible for evaluating the school guidance programme. The counsellor is also expected to read and interpret literature to apply research findings to everyday counsels' situations and to improve his or her skills continuously through evaluation of counselling techniques.

The counsellor responsibilities identified by Schafer and Mufson would likely be found in the large majority of school districts across the nation. Within the area of assessment, roles include test interpreter, test developer, evaluator of programmes, consultant, and researcher. Several studies reviewed by Schafer and Mufson were supportive of these roles.

Counselling for Children from Broken Family

Children's reactions depend on their age and developmental stage at the time the divorce occurs.

Early Latency (ages 5-8). Children between the ages of five and eight at the time of their parents' divorce tend to react with great sadness. Some may feel fearful, insecure, helpless, and abandoned by the missing parent. Younger children often express guilt and blame themselves for their parents' divorce.

Late Latency (ages 9-12). Children in late latency at the time of their parents' divorce are distinguished from younger children by their feelings of intense anger. Nine to 12-year-olds may still feel loneliness, loss, shock, surprise, and fear, but anger and possibly the rejection of one parent are the predominant reactions of this age group.

Adolescence (ages 13-18). Adolescents whose parents are divorcing also experience loss, sadness, anger, and pain. A typical adolescent reaction to parental divorce, however, often involves acting-out behaviours. Sexual promiscuity, delinquency, the use of alcohol and drugs, and aggressive behaviour have all been identified as adolescent reactions to parental divorce.

In Wallerstein and Kelly's five-year longitudinal study of 60 families and 131 children of divorce, teachers reported that two-thirds of the children showed changes in school behaviour and/or academic performance following the parental separation. Cantrell concurs that teachers frequently report observing changes in academic achievement, moods, attendance patterns, and behaviour of children adjusting to their parents' divorce.

Responsibilities of School

The school is in an excellent position to offer supportive services to children of divorce. Children spend much time in school, where the continuity and routine can offer a safe environment for interventions. Counsellors, teachers, and other school personnel are available on a daily basis and can provide help that avoids both the stigma and the expense associated with seeking help form private practitioners. Finally, the number of children in the school provides the possibility for group interventions.

The school counsellor can provide valuable assistance directly through counselling with the children and indirectly through services to school administrators, teachers, and parents. Scherman and Lepak suggest that counsellors not view divorce as a single problem with negative consequences, but focus on changes caused by divorce (e.g., single-parent homes, changes in routines and life stlyes, visitation patterns with relatives) and their positive, negative, or neutral effects on the children.

Working with administrators: Drake identified 10 major issues facing administrators with regard to children of divorce: school territorial rights, parental access to school records, release of the child from school, school visits, medical emergencies, financial responsibility, the child's surname, retention, confidentiality of records, and parental access to school functions. Counsellors can consult with school administrators on these policy issues and help them to understand the legal implications of divorce for the school. Because kidnapping of a child by the noncustodial parent may be a concern, schools need to guard against the possibility of parental kidnapping. Burns and Brassard suggest that schools:

1. Ask parents to inform the school about custody concerns.
2. Require parents to show legal documentation of sole custody when they report a sole custody arrangement.
3. Ensure that teachers are aware of custody status.
4. Maintain an office list of children and custodial parents.

Working with Teachers: School counsellors can help teachers and other school personnel by conducting in-services on the effects of divorce on children and their classroom behaviour.

Counsellors can also help to sensitise teachers to the transition a child is experiencing and to the implications of that transition. Teachers may need to change their choice of words, or to adapt their curriculum and classroom resource materials to include various family types.

Working with Parents: Counsellors can make parents aware of the special needs of their child during the divorce transition. A study by Hammond of third- to sixth-graders, for example, revealed that 74 percent of the 82 children who were from separated or divorced families believed that school counsellors could help by talking with parents of children who asked the counsellor to do so. Counsellors can also assist parents by referring them to divorce support groups in the community, by recommending reading materials that deal with families of divorce, and by suggesting ways that parents can help their children adjust to divorce.

Working with Children: Intervention strategies with children will depend on each child's individual needs. Kieffer suggests an adaptation of Kelly and Wallerstein's Divorce Specific Assessment which involves determining the child's developmental achievements, interviewing the child about his/her response to the family situation, and evaluating the child's existing support systems.

Hammond's study found that over 86 percent of third- to sixth-graders interviewed thought that counsellors could best help children whose parents are divorcing by encouraging the children to talk about their feelings. Approximately the same percentage reported that counsellors could also help by providing children with books to read about divorce.

Individual Counselling. Although there exists little research testing the efficacy of individual counselling with children of divorce, clinicians report a desirable change in the child's affect as a result of individual counselling. Individual counselling is usually reserved for children with long-term, unproductive coping behaviours and for children who cannot work well in groups.

Group Counselling: Robson reports that children's groups on divorce, led by elementary school counsellors with specific strategies to meet the needs of these children, have been extremely successful. Divorce groups are a popular choice for counsellors because of their cost effectiveness and multiple benefits. Eighty-two percent of the students in Hammond's study reported that a group counselling situation for children would be beneficial.

Cantrell suggests that counsellors using group counselling with children of divorce deal with the developmental responses of the children while helping them to label and understand their feelings, realise that others are having similar feelings and experiences, understand the divorce process, learn new coping skills, and feel good about themselves and their parents. Several types of group counselling are available which could be beneficial to children of divorce:

1. Situational/transitional groups offer emotional support; catharsis; and information sharing about stress, mutual feelings, and similar experiences.
2. Structured groups can teach children how to deal with crisis situations through group discussions, role playing, and the use of drawings and collages.
3. One-day workshops for children between the ages of 10 and 17 can use sentence completion exercises, assertiveness training, and films about divorce to help group members explore values and assumptions about

marriage and divorce, learn to express and cope with their own and their parents' feelings, and develop communication skills for handling difficult situations.

Valuing Diversity in the Schools

The valuing of diversity in the schools is no longer merely a social goal. With the make-up of the student body changing so rapidly, school counsellors, teachers and administrators realise that they are now required to learn new techniques and skills for understanding, motivating, teaching, and empowering each individual student regardless of race, gender, religion or creed. We are a nation of diverse populations and groups.

The future of our society depends upon our ability to effectively talk with one another, to reach mutual understanding, and to realise that in diversity there is strength. School counsellors can serve as catalysts to insure that teachers, students and others learn how to value diversity. That is, the valuing of diversity can be taught to others and should be a major part of any school's comprehensive guidance programme.

Valuing Diversity Model

The "A" in ASK stands for Awareness of self and others. Self and other awareness is a must if cultural diversity is to be appreciated in our schools and elsewhere. The "S" in ASK refers to both Sensitivity and Skills. Sensitivity to others as well as new, innovative, communication. Skills are needed by students and others if we are to learn to value diversity and intercultural communication is to improve. The "K" stands for Knowledge of cultures different from our own. Culture influences feelings, thoughts, non-verbal behaviours, ideas and perceptions and "cognitive empathy" (knowledge) of another's culture is needed to improve intercultural relationships.

Self-awareness

Self-aware individuals avoid a condescending attitude and do not patronise culturally different persons. To patronise implies the belief that we hold a superior position to them—we come across to them as being "better" than they. And members of other cultural groups view this as disrespectful. Relatedly, some Anglo Americans seem to have a characteristic that could best be described as "assumed similarity." That is, they assume that people either ought to be like them or want to be like them! Self-aware individuals do not hold such assumptions. Students of all ages can be taught, through various guidance and counselling activities, to be more aware of self and others.

Sensitivity and Communication Skills

Our sensitivity toward and willingness to understand others is a major key to effective communication with the culturally different. We need to be aware of others' thoughts and feelings, regardless of their race, creed or cultural background. Effective, multicultural communicators are aware of other persons' frames of reference, their views of the world. And, they understand that worldviews are influenced by culture. We can learn communication skills that will assist us in understanding how others view their worlds and react to them, as opposed to telling them how they should react and behave toward their own worlds! Their worldviews may be very different from ours, but they are based on their perceptions—which are their "realities." And, their reality determines how they feel, think and behave.

How sensitive are you to your own views of those who are different? Do you view other cultures as equally valuable to yours? Is your cultural group superior to another? Are you culturally sensitive to your own heritage and the possibility that you were taught (perhaps unconsciously) to be prejudiced as a part of your upbringing? Do you value and respect differences? Are you aware of your own values and biases and how they affect those who are culturally different? Do you avoid stereotyping and labelling? Do you monitor your own assumptions about those different from you? Are you willing to accept someone of a different race into your organisation, i.e., your sorority, your fraternity, your church? It is important that each of us examine ourselves concerning these questions if we hope to become culturally skilled communicators.

The emerging sense of worth of members of culturally distinct populations can no longer be neglected. Learning about their different values, attitudes, desires, aspirations, and beliefs is necessary because it affects all of us. Learning skills to help us communicate effectively with people from different cultures will speed up this necessary learning process.

Feelings, thoughts, nonverbal behaviours, and ideas are important in interpersonal communication and are culturally influenced and learned. Empathy, interest in others, caring, personal awareness, sensitivity and understanding are stressed as important to effective interpersonal communication and to learning to value diversity. However, having these core conditions present is not always enough for effective communication with a person from another race or culture. We also need "cognitive" empathy. That is, knowledge of that person's culture, or knowing "where that person is coming from" is also extremely important.

Students of all ages can be taught to be culturally skilled. A culturally skilled communicator is willing to gain cognitive knowledge about different cultures, i.e., their history, cultural values, current problems and lifestyles and how this impacts on their respective worldview. This may be the most important thing we can do in becoming more effective intercultural communicators. Having strong feelings of support for a particular culture and its participants is necessary.

However, it is not enough to truly communicate with participants from that cultural group. If we are ignorant of the values and ways of participants from cultural groups different from ours, we will certainly be less effective communicators than we would be if we operated with accurate, cognitive understanding of them. The teaching of the values and ways of other cultural groups can, and should be, central to any comprehensive school guidance programme.

Model Implementation

The professional school counsellor possesses many excellent communication skills that can, and should be, shared and taught to teachers, administrators, students, and others. The "cognitive knowledge" aspect of the above described model can easily be generalised to the school setting. There are many effective ways that students can obtain knowledge about others' cultures, e.g., outside speakers from different cultural backgrounds, culturally distinct student panels, field trips, etc. Learning about other cultures should be a major component of any guidance curriculum, regardless of the school level.

In addition, self awareness, awareness of others and sensitivity to self and others in regard to diversity can and should be a major component of any comprehensive school guidance programme. Many guidance activities can be developed and delivered by various modes with these themes in mind. School counsellors know how to communicate effectively with others regardless of their or the other person's cultural background. They are skilled in how to "tune in to" the feelings of others, how to put the speaker at ease by clarifying the content of what was just said, how to show interest in others through the use of open-ended questions, etc. And the research is clear, these skills can be taught to students of all ages, i.e., there is considerable evidence that peers can become very effective in helping other peers. And, through structured guidance and counselling approaches all students and teachers can be taught these facilitative communication skills.

3

Secondary School Counsellor

More and more children and youth are coming to school with serious personal problems. In schools, the individuals trained to help students deal with their personal problems are school counsellors.

Responsibilities of Secondary School Counsellors

Several influences have impacted what has been referred to as "the role" of secondary school counsellors. Among the influences are state certification standards; counsellor education training programmes; the nature of school systems; professional organisations; principals and other administrators' beliefs about counsellors; and the counsellors themselves. Principals have had a major influence on counsellors' roles. In many situations, principals have dictated "the role" by assigning the counsellor "duties"—often administrative or quasi-administrative duties (e.g., counting credits, keeping track of attendance, discipline) that have little to do with the actual role of school counsellors or the needs of students.

School counsellors appear to be reluctant or unable to convince principals that they should perform the duties for which they have been trained. This must change if school counsellors are to have any influence in the restructured schools of the future. In this complex and troubled society, school counsellors are being asked to assume a greater role in the lives of their students and the students' families. The challenges facing counsellors and demands on their time will continue to grow during the next decade.

School counsellors must choose carefully where they spend their time and energy. But, given the challenges faced by today's students, school counsellors must focus on students' personal/social, educational, and career needs. In order to do so, counsellors need to move from a services-oriented approach (orientation, information, assessment, counselling, placement, and follow-up) to a school counselling programme approach. They must be clear about their "scope of practice" – the responsibilities for which they are trained – and not allow themselves to become assistant principals, attendance officers, substitute teachers, and clerks.

School counsellors can exert more control over their scope of practice if they commit themselves to designing and implementing developmental school counselling programmes. While crisis and remedial counselling will always be a part of the school counsellor's responsibilities, counsellors must provide assistance to as many students as possible. Emphasising developmental counselling programmes permits counsellors to be seen as contributing to the growth of all students and not just working with those "in trouble."

Developmental counselling programmes focus on meeting students' needs and lead to activities and structured group experiences for all students. They are proactive rather than reactive and when counsellors are busy implementing their programme, they are unavailable for unrelated administrative and clerical duties. Developmental Counselling Programmes include both "content" and "process" components. The content component of the programme speaks to:

1. The rationale for the programme (why the school and children need a counselling programme);
2. The personal-social, educational, and career development skills or competencies needed by children and youth; and
3. The management plan or blueprint intended to guide counsellors' management of the counselling programme.

The process component includes:

1. The activities counsellors will use to help students achieve the designated skills or competencies;
2. The counselling strategies they intend to employ, e.g., individual counselling, group counselling, classroom guidance, and/or consultation; and
3. Methods to be used to evaluate their programme and improve their effectiveness with students, staff, and parents.

In a comprehensive developmental school counselling programme, the counsellor has the following scope of practice (the responsibilities for which a school counsellor is trained and qualified):

Design. Counsellors design the content of the programme. Gysbers, refers to this content as a "guidance curriculum." The content of the programme is designed to help students gain skills or competencies in personal-social, educational, and career domains. Following is a list of skills/competencies that one might expect to see in the content of a developmental counselling programme.

1. Personal-Social Skills. Students will:
   - (a) gain self-awareness and improve self-esteem;
   - (b) make healthy choices and effective decisions;
   - (c) assume responsibility for their own behaviour;
   - (d) respect individual differences and cooperate; and
   - (e) learn to resolve conflicts.
2. Educational Skills. Students will:
   - (a) acquire study and test-taking skills;
   - (b) seek and use educational information;
   - (c) set educational goals; and
   - (d) make appropriate educational choices.
3. Career Development Skills. Students will:
   - (a) analyse interests, aptitudes, and skills;
   - (b) recognise effects of career stereotyping;
   - (c) form a career identity; and
   - (d) plan for their future careers.

Delivery. Counsellors must be involved in the delivery of this developmental programme content or curriculum that they have developed. They must allocate significant amounts of time to facilitate or team teach developmental learning activities in the classrooms. Also, they will need to set up inservices for teachers to enable them to assist in the facilitation of the activities. Counsellors need to deliver their programme content in small and large group sessions. Large group sessions may be appropriate for the information about and discussion of post-secondary or vocational education options and financial aid. Small groups may be more appropriate for interests or aptitude test interpretations.

Counsel. Counsellors must counsel students both individually and in small groups. Counsellors must not forget their unique counselling skills. While schools are not appropriate cites for "caseloads of clients," counsellors must always allot time for counselling students with personal-social problems, both individually and in small groups. In order to be as effective as possible in a limited number of sessions, counsellors should utilise newer theoretical approaches such as brief therapy.

Consult. Counsellors must consult with parents, teachers, other educators, and various community agencies to help students deal with more serious personal and educational problems, both individually and in small groups. In order to be as effective as possible, in a limited number of sessions, counsellors should utilise newer theoretical approaches such as brief therapy.

Coordinate. Counsellors must coordinate or collaborate with others who may be offering mental health-oriented programmes, e.g., substance abuse. Counsellors report that more and more community-based programmes are operating in the schools. The school counsellors should either coordinate the efforts of these programmes or collaborate in their delivery. Testing programmes are often coordinated by school counsellors. In these days of accountability, counsellors must be careful not to permit this responsibility to consume too much of their time. While counsellors should understand thoroughly all relevant interest, aptitude, and achievement tests and should be able to offer inservices to teachers on their interpretation and use, they should not be spending their time in direct administration of tests.

Manage. Counsellors must manage the school counselling programme. Directors of guidance are a dying breed. Many counsellors find themselves supervised by individuals who have more responsibilities than they can handle. Counsellors must take charge of their own programmes and encourage interaction and regular meetings of the counsellors in their district in order to assure programme progress. Managing a school counselling programme includes developing an active staff/community public relations programme.

Counsellors should orient staff and community to the counselling programme through newsletters, local media, and school and community presentations. Managing also involves pulling together advisory committees of parents and community members to gather input related to student needs. The management function is critical to the success of a school counselling programme.

Evaluate. Counsellors need to evaluate their efforts with students, staff, and community. Counsellors can gather evaluation data from several sources. One source of information is "general evaluation" data which includes number of students seen in individual or crisis counselling, number of small group counselling sessions, number of large group information sessions, number of conferences with parents, and number of phone calls to parents and community agencies. While this kind of general evaluation does not speak to the quality of counsellor contacts, it does provide the school board and administration information about the scope or breadth of the counselling programme.

"Specific evaluation" data takes more counsellor planning time. Counsellors need to plan to evaluate their work with students (particularly the delivery of the guidance activities in classrooms). Ratings scales to be completed by teachers and/or students and short surveys to determine what students gained from the guidance activities are two additional methods that can be used to evaluate the counselling programme. Programme evaluation is one of the weakest areas in school counselling. Many counsellors will need to seek assistance from nearby counsellor educators in setting up their evaluation process.

Responsibilities of Elementary School Counsellor

Our society faces challenges in accepting and benefiting from cultural diversity. Problems emanating from racism exist despite efforts aimed at educational reform. Elementary school counsellors must be aware of transmitting their own cultural values to children and of drawing erroneous conclusions about children's emotional and social well-being based on cultural differences.

Moreover, because counselling theories and techniques are not always applicable across cultures, counsellors must often look to new and creative ways to work effectively in multicultural settings. Elementary school counsellors should advocate for educational programmes that include counsellors, teachers, parents, and students working together for increased cultural understanding through role playing and other awareness activities.

The so-called traditional family has virtually disappeared in America. Divorce and single-parent homes are a fact of life confronting children. Elementary school counsellors must understand the effects of changing family structures and find ways to promote child growth and development within the context of family change. These ways will include divorce groups, training groups for single parents, guidance for latchkey children, and a variety of other important strategies.

Elementary school counsellors need to develop innovative approaches to help children and parents develop in a healthy fashion in spite of the ambiguity created by divorce and single-parent families. Counsellors should assume a proactive stance by collaborating with teachers in developing and implementing family education programmes.

Students often begin to experiment with drugs in elementary school and early experimentation frequently leads to abuse and addiction in adolescence. Moreover, educators are aware of problems coming from families made dysfunctional by alcoholism and drug addiction. Elementary school counsellors must understand the scope and implications of substance abuse and implement drug education programmes that are designed to prevent drug abuse and to help children overcome the effects of substance abuse in their families. Elementary school counsellors also need to recognise the serious effects of parents' alcoholism on children's development and implement compassionate approaches to helping these young victims receive help whether or not their parents are willing to accept help.

Child abuse and neglect are rampant in our society. Elementary school counsellors can build a positive school environment for youngsters who suffer from abuse and neglect by implementing such programmes as parent support groups to prevent physical abuse of children, programmes that help identify potential child abusers, and preventive sexual abuse programmes. Elementary school counsellors cannot work alone in preventing and treating child abuse. They need to develop close working relationships with social services and other community agencies that frequently advocate for victims of abuse and neglect.

Counsellors also need to work closely with teachers to help them thoroughly understand signs of abuse and to acquaint them with correct referral procedures. The elementary school classroom may be the most stable setting neglected and abused children experience and may provide the empathy and positive regard needed to help children cope with their ordeal. Elementary school counsellors must, therefore, become increasingly sensitive to the victims of abuse and to the need for effective counselling programmes in this troublesome area.

Many children in our schools are labelled exceptional and find it difficult to accept that they are "simply human." These children need to feel accepted and to use their exceptional characteristics in extraordinary ways. Children who are not so labelled need to learn ways of benefiting from those who are exceptional. The parents and teachers of exceptional children also need to find ways to understand and assist these youngsters. Elementary school counsellors should work to build a supportive learning environment for exceptional children. There is a need for strong ties between counselling and special education.

Counsellors should develop programmes for parents of exceptional children. Parents of gifted youngsters, for example, have unique needs resulting from misunderstandings created by myths, stereotypes, and the small number of gifted children in the population. Counsellors should also develop strategies to help teachers work more effectively with parents of handicapped children because the teacher is in a position to develop an active, ongoing relationship with parents but may lack the training to provide effective counselling support.

Technological advances have changed education, work, and leisure in our society. Although most people experience the benefits of these advances, most also know the anxiety and frustration that accompany rapid technological change as well as the alienation generated by impersonal aspects of technology. Elementary school counsellors need to help children develop emotionally and socially in the context of rapid technological change. Counsellors often need to deal first with their own concerns about technology before helping children understand the benefits and limitations of technology. Elementary school counsellors especially need to acquire competencies with computers, to overcome anxieties about using the technology, and to integrate computer technology into counselling programmes.

Elementary school counsellors face major challenges as they work with parents and teachers to introduce children to an ever-changing world of work. The emphasis on career education, however, seems to have diminished from its peak in the 1970s when the United States Office of Education demanded high visibility for career education programmes in schools. This decline in career education at the elementary school level is unfortunate because economic, political, and social changes have brought women and minorities into the work force in large numbers and have altered how children must be prepared to enter the world of work. Elementary school counsellors need to enhance children's career awareness, prevent sex-role stereotyping through career exploration programmes, and use role models to expand children's occupational aspirations.

American society has placed increasing emphasis on the need for children to learn basic academic skills. Parents throughout the country complain that children are not learning to read, write, and perform basic mathematics.

Governmental and private commissions have studied the poor academic achievement of children and are asking educators to account for the failure of our schools in this important area. If elementary school counsellors are to fulfil their mission in schools, they must collaborate with teachers, parents, and school administrators in an effort to improve children's achievement.

Elementary school counsellors can positively effect children's achievement. Counsellors, for example, can implement and evaluate a ten-session programme called "Succeeding in School". Counsellors can also consult with parents on matters related to children's academic progress, implement classroom programmes that improve the work habits of children who procrastinate with school work, and use group counselling as a means of motivating children to attend school.

Children's behaviour, both in and out of school, is an important concern of parents and educators. The popular media has documented seemingly wide-spread school absenteeism and delinquency among our nation's youth. How to change children's misbehaviour and to foster productive behaviour are concerns of elementary school counsellors. The techniques available to parents, teachers, and elementary school counsellors for managing children's behaviour are numerous and include modelling, positive reinforcement, behaviour contracting, and desensitisation. These behavioural change procedures have been thoroughly tested.

Although the application of these methods is often difficult, the collaborative efforts of elementary school counsellors, teachers, and parents in applying behavioural techniques eases some of the difficulties and increases the chances of success. Counselling interventions to improve behaviour include classroom guidance sessions, small group counselling sessions, and consultation with teachers. Students who receive a combination of these treatment procedures are likely to behave well in the classroom and elsewhere.

Children need to support each other in a world filled with conflict. They must learn and practice the interpersonal skills necessary for their present lives and also for the demands of peer pressure in adolescence. Elementary school counsellors must find ways both to challenge and support youngsters in the area of human relations. Counsellors can build positive relationships among children and between children and adults through affective education programmes in the classroom and through innovative approaches to peer counselling.

Elementary school counsellors play a major part in developing and maintaining a healthy social climate for children. This aspect of counsellors' work is important in part because children's relations with teachers, peers, and family affect learning and achievement. In addition, counsellors who strive to improve children's interpersonal skills are helping to ensure that the 1990s and beyond will be years in which society will move forward on the basis of cooperative efforts among the nation's citizens. Finally, the work of elementary school counsellors in this area will likely help to produce citizens who strive for productive relations across cultures and nations.

Responsibilities of Professional School Counsellors

Home education, also called homeschooling or home school, is the process by which children are educated at home rather than at an institution such as a public or private school. Prior to the introduction of compulsory school attendance in the 19th century, most education worldwide occurred within the family and community, with only a small proportion of the population attending schools or employing tutors.

Lyman offered the following reasons people choose homeschooling: religious values in education; worries over crime and lack of discipline in public schools; concern about the quality of education; and the belief that children are best educated by parents. Lange and Liu, in a study of homeschooling in Minnesota, found similarly that "special needs of the children, educational philosophy, parenting style and religious and ethical beliefs" were factors in choosing to homeschool.

McDowell offered a different perspective with an epidemiological approach to analysing the incidents of violence on the homeschooling movement. She determined that the influence of homeschooling along with the negative factors associated with public schools multiplied the number of persons who participated in homeschooling. Kozlowski addressed reasons for homeschooling by superintendents and parents in Alabama. The superintendents reported that shielding children from adverse social factors and inculcating morals and values were the parents' most frequent reasons for homeschooling. The parents on the other hand stated "individual attention and raising confident, caring and well-rounded people" as their reasons.

Families who homeschool their children generally can be described as religious, conservative, college educated, middle-class, two parent, and politically active. Bauman concluded that homeschooling families are most prevalent in rural and suburban areas of the West and tend to have one parent not in the labour force. Rudner revealed that about one-fourth of homeschooled students were being educated by a parent who was a certified teacher. In terms of achievement, Rudner found that about 25% of homeschoolers were performing at one or more grade levels above their peers in public and private schools.

Public schools have long had connections with the homeschool community via services such as part-time enrolment and participation in student activities. A public school in Barnstable, Massachusetts helped to pioneer the concept of assistance to homeschool families as early as 1978. In addition, the Cupertino Union School District in California provided open enrolment/alternative education beginning in 1975. One notable public school system connecting with homeschoolers is the Federal Way School District in Washington.

The Federal Way School District instituted an Internet academy that provides instruction through on-line courses, chat rooms, e-mail and phone support from supervising district teachers. Homeschool students can attend courses but also have the option to enroll for all instruction on-line. Those without computer access can utilise a school district computer lab or computers at public libraries. As school districts have opened their doors to homeschooled children in the areas of curricular and extracurricular activities, legal concerns have been raised with regard to the requests for services. Controversy has centered on the eligibility requirements for participation in sports programmes. School counsellors should be aware of the ways in which connections between public schools and the homeschool community continue to evolve.

One of the primary reasons for building partnerships with the homeschooling population is to serve students, which is consistent with the public school mission to provide "quality educational experiences for all school-aged children". Other reasons include the requirements of state legislation, funding that may be available for serving homeschooled children as a result of state guidelines, and "maintaining positive working relationships with students who may eventually re-enroll in the school". In rural settings, the appeal for school counselling services may be greater since alternative options for services may not be available.

Given the sparsity of research dedicated to the involvement of homeschooled children in school counselling programmes, the following recommendations are offered.

First, school counselling sponsored services such as college nights, career fairs, college admissions counselling, financial aid and scholarship information, standardised testing, test preparation sessions, access to Advanced Placement classes and other enrichment activities should be made available to the homeschooling population. In addition to these services, many school counselling programmes offer computerised career development programmes that could assist homeschooled students in identifying career fields and potential college majors. Not surprisingly this latter point is of interest to homeschoolers as many will seek admission to college.

Second, as a strategy to further involve the home school population within school counselling programmes, efforts can be made to include a home schooling advocate on school counselling advisory councils. Carney reported that a critical component of comprehensive competency-based guidance models is the advisory council that assists in the evaluation and enhancement of the school counselling programme. These councils usually consist of a broad range of individuals and include representation from ethnic minority groups, persons with disabilities, and persons of various ages. A homeschooling representative would help keep the public school counsellors in touch with the needs of homeschoolers.

Third, many school counselling programmes list the types of services that they provide on a school district or school website. This practice is beneficial to inform home school populations of the services offered. It also allows them to select the services that they desire. Publicising school activities and programmes in homeschooling resources would further encourage the involvement of homeschooled children.

Fourth, participation in school counselling programmes could assist homeschoolers in obtaining letters of recommendation from school counsellors. Since many of these students have to submit a detailed portfolio of experiences for college admissions in order to be recognised as a competitive applicant, the letters of recommendation from school counsellors could prove to be useful.

Fifth, counsellors can provide homeschooling parents information on child development, student learning, curriculum planning, assessment and evaluation. Other support services that would be beneficial are administering achievement tests and proctoring exams.

A trend has been established for public schools to provide services to homeschoolers. As services are extended to this new and growing population, school counsellors will be challenged to develop relationships and make positive connections with homeschoolers. These connections fit the mission of public education and also create relationships with students who may at some point become full-time clients on school counsellors' caseloads.

4

High School Counselling

High School Guidance Counsellors deliver the comprehensive guidance programme to students in grades nine through twelve in a manner that prepares students for post secondary opportunities. High School Counsellors must have the following qualifications,

– are professional educators,

– have earned a Master's Degree,

– are specifically trained in counselling techniques,

– are certified as school counsellors by the Texas Education Agency.

High School Counsellors address their continuing professional growth through:

– Inservice training

– Workshops

– Local, state and national conferences

– Continuing Education

– Inter-school counsellor meetings

– Current professional literature and media information

- Presentations to professional groups
- Technology networking

Students may see the school counsellor through...

- A student self referral
- A teacher referral
- A parent referral
- A counsellor request
- An administrator request

Students may want to see the counsellor for many reasons, including assistance with:

- Problem-solving by exploring alternatives to make appropriate decisions.
- Developing positive attitudes towards self and others.
- Establishing personal goals.
- Developing educational plans and in selecting the related courses based on individual interests and talents.
- Interpretation of results of standardised tests.

High School Counsellors across the district provide similar services tailored to the educational level and to the student and campus needs. High School Counsellors teach the guidance curriculum and assist teachers with guidance-related curricula. The following are examples of the topics that are addressed in class guidance sessions.

- Academic support
- Career pathways
- Character development

- Decision-making
- Developmental assets
- Goal-Setting
- Graduation requirements
- Study skills
- Understanding academic records
- Conflict management

High School Counsellors provide individual or group assistance with educational planning and career exploration. Sample activities include the following:

- 9-12 Pre-registration activities such as course selection and review of graduation requirements.
- Special events such as college and career days, financial aid programmes and elective fairs.
- Assistance to students with information for special programmes such as dual credit, transition/IEP needs.
- Student/parent conferences to address educational and career planning.
- Freshman Conferences to orient students to high school.
- Sophomore conferences to review student Graduation Status Report (GSR), to interpret the standardised test scores and to provide career guidance.
- Junior Conferences to review the GSR, to provide college, career and relevant testing information.
- Senior Conferences to review the GSR, provide post-secondary education admissions information, as well as scholarship and financial aid information.

High School Counsellors provide students with counselling services, either individually or in groups, to address relevant adolescent issues as a result of student, teacher, parent and/or administrator concerns, or for crisis response. Examples of concerns students may bring to the counsellor's office include the following:

– Conflict mediation
– Dropout prevention
– Financial assistance
– Peer relations
– Progress toward graduation
– Schedule issues or changes
– Social issues
– Teen parenting
– Violence and drug abuse issues

Counsellors also provide consultation services to parents and teachers. Additionally, counsellors may refer students (and when needed, their families) to other programmes for other resources or services such as:

– Safe and Drug Free Programme,
– Gifted and Talented Programme,
– Special Education Services,
– HORIZONS Programme, (perhaps link to their website)
– Other district and community resources and services.

High School Counsellors coordinate with school and community to bring together resources for students. Counsellors provide information about:

– AP Testing Schedule
– Exit Level TAAS testing schedule
– Scholastic Aptitude Test (SAT) and American College Testing (ACT) testing schedule and preparatory classes
– PSAT Test Schedule

Counsellors organise or assist with many activities on behalf of students with other campus, district and community groups. Counsellors provide consultation and training services to school staff and parents. Topics they address can include the following:

– Developmental Assets
– Multicultural/Diversity training
– Guidance programme information
– New teacher training
– Signs and symptoms of substance abuse and violence

Counselling for Hispanic Students

Based on cultural stereotypes about Hispanic students, many teachers see lower potential and expect lower performance. In a study of Mexican-American students, teachers were more likely to show disapproval toward Spanish-dominant than English-dominant students and to attribute negative characteristics to students who spoke accented or nonstandard English or nonstandard Spanish.

Another study found that teachers attributed such negative characteristics as low social status, low educational attainment, and low intelligence to Hispanic students who had accents or who were nonstandard speakers. A United States Commission on Civil Rights study showed that teachers direct praise or encouragement at Anglo students 36 percent more often than at Mexican-American students; build on the spoken contribution of Anglo students 40 percent more often; and ask Anglo students 20 percent more questions than they ask Mexican-American students.

Test Performance

A number of factors clearly depress the test performance of Hispanic students. First, the lower socioeconomic and educational level of Hispanic families generally correlates with low test performance, regardless of ethnicity. Second are problems within the testing situation: cultural differences, which hinder guessing or interpretation; text anxiety; a relatively slower speed of test taking that decreases chances of test completion; unfamiliarity with the accepted nuance of test vocabulary; and, possibly, culturally different test-taking strategies. According to Duran,

> Neither high school grades nor admissions test scores alone or in combination ought to bear the sole burden of evidence for making decisions to admit Hispanic-background students to college.... Admissions personnel need to be provided with a broader range of information on Hispanics' background, language, and culture in weighing admissions decisions.

Hispanic students rely less on their guidance counsellors and parents for career information than do other groups of students and, instead, resort more frequently to books, magazines, and former students, as well as classroom teachers, librarians and career specialists. Hispanics also tend to be more vulnerable to both the positive and negative influences of school personnel than are middle-class, non-Hispanic White youth. Though research on counselling

Hispanics is scarce, existing research indicates that what counsellors fail to do is just as significant as what they do.

In interviews, Puerto Rican students cited counsellors' failure to explain adequately the college-going process as preventing these students from applying to colleges. High schools that are successful in getting Hispanics into college combine a number of strategies:

- High expectations and a strong academic curriculum challenge both teachers and students and have far-reaching effects.
- Early identification of college-bound students enhances chances for better preparation. But early identification should not be rigid, should avoid tracking, and the selection of college-bound students should not be left entirely to school personnel, or be based entirely on test scores and grades. Given a proper explanation of the expectations and responsibilities, students should be allowed to enter the college process at any point in their high school careers.
- A well-developed information system needs to alert students about visits from college recruiters, test deadlines, college days/nights, college fairs, college orientation days, scholarship deadlines, and other events. Teachers need to be attuned to these activities in order to plan lessons accordingly and to provide assistance whenever necessary. Parents need to be aware in order to provide a role of support and encouragement. And counsellors need to be sensitive to the community's language preference—and to accept the fact that some information may need to be disseminated in both Spanish and English.
- An organised effort to prepare students for standardised testing, college admission, and financial

aid application is essential. Students need not only information on deadlines and visits, but an understanding of their importance in getting into college. Activities should be designed to help students successfully complete each step.

– A well-defined role for resource groups, including parents, teachers, college recruiters, ex-students, and community organisations, should be creatively designed to fit the needs of the individual school.

Precollege Guidance and Counselling

Studies show that the greatest determinant of who goes to college is socioeconomic status. Parents and counsellors are the primary influences. The decision is very different for first- and second-generation college entrants. Students who are most likely to depend on the school are those whose parents have not experienced college. Lee and Ekstrom report that 56 percent of public high school students report some counsellor influence; this is particularly true for blacks, females, students in the academic track, and those who plan to attend four-year colleges.

Counsellors play a crucial role in the student's passage through the educational process. They facilitate decision-making and access to appropriate courses and experiences to help students address immediate and long-term goals. In public schools, scheduling and discipline take precedence over precollege counselling in the use of counsellors' time. Though the student to counsellor ratio limits the practical availability of counselling, Chapman and DeMasi indicate that 20 percent of counsellor time is used for college advising and that counsellors report satisfaction with this situation.

In some studies, precollege advising has come under a great deal of criticism. Though students appreciate counsellors' functioning in other spheres, Chapman and others found low-income students indifferent to the counsellor's role in assisting with postsecondary preparation. College advising by the school counsellor is especially important in low-income and minority families where parents are unable to offer first-hand information on college life, selection, and financial aid. Chapman and others and Lee and Ekstrom, however, found that counsellors often devote more time to college-bound, middle- and upper-income white students. Though blacks have significantly more counsellor contacts than others (mostly regarding financial aid), in general, low-income students do not use counsellors as much as other students do.

Family income is the major determinant of the education a student receives. Counsellors are in a position to help overcome the considerable inequities evident in education, provided that school systems give them the support and resources necessary to carry out their responsibilities.

Lee and Ekstrom, on examination of the national longitudinal database in U.S., HIGH SCHOOL AND BEYOND, found differential access to counselling by socioeconomic status, race/ethnicity, aspiration level and ability. Also pertinent were size and location of schools, school resources, and expectations of the community. Access to counselling is thus acting as a social stratifier, possibly magnifying the differences in outcomes of secondary schooling. Students planning to attend college are more likely to seek counselling for planning their high school programmes than are students without aspirations for higher education. Hispanics, whose attrition rate is particularly high and whose expectations of success in completing college are low, make less use of counselling services.

Students who lack access to counselling are more likely to be placed in the nonacademic curriculum track. Counselling for tracking is necessary at the beginning of a student's high school career, and neglect in this area has caused many students, especially minorities and low-income students, to lack adequate preparation for postsecondary education, thus perpetuating a situation of disadvantage. Choice of track is also tied into expectations. Vocational-track students presumably take coursework to match their career plans, but general track students have the least focus in their curricular programmes and require correspondingly more assistance in making wise choices regarding appropriate employment or continuation of education.

The Commission on Precollege Guidance and Counselling recommends that less talented students need to be in more flexible programmes, moving up as competency improves and is demonstrated. Counselling must interpret to all students what is necessary for postsecondary educational access in order to help students overcome socioeconomic barriers.

Timelines in Counselling

1. The Elementary Years: Work with parents on supporting students' belief in their own capabilities.
2. Middle or Junior High School:
   - Develop aspirations and sustain motivation;
   - promote effective study skills (notetaking, memorising, etc.);

– aid in clarification of values, decision-making;
– differentiate among programmes and courses, clarifying consequences of choices;
– discuss graduation requirements, electives, required courses;
– review testing history, decide on levels of secondary subjects;
– schedule subjects (family decision) based on testing and academic experiences;
– introduce guidance resources – counselling services, guidebooks and publications, computer programmes, and video systems; and
– suggest the possibility of college and the availability of financial aid.

3. Ninth Grade:
– Schedule family meetings and individual conferences on course decisions;
– present resource materials;
– provide access to academic, career, and vocational counselling;
– organise group meetings, college and career planning nights;
– review academic progress, determine future course selection; and
– counsel for study skills (time management, memory improvement, filing, and retrieving information).

4. Tenth Grade:
– Schedule family meetings on course selection, review of future plans and academic progress;

- organise group meetings on college/career, financing college education;
- encourage students to meet college representatives, attend college fairs, career programmes, financial aid workshops;
- provide guidance regarding goal-setting, decision-making, interview skills, testing skills;
- conduct a writing and speaking curriculum unit;
- assist in college planning—have students learn about tests, take PSAT/SAT, meet with counsellors for test interpretation, obtain counsel regarding test-taking techniques;
- advise college contacts—visiting college representatives, attending college days, college fairs, career programmes; and
- suggest students write for college materials.

5. Eleventh Grade:
   - Schedule family meetings on course selection, level determination, postsecondary plans/provisional college choices, planning for college, visiting colleges, financial aid;
   - provide testing and interpretation of results;
   - participate in college search;
   - assist early financial planning activity;
   - recommend students visit college representatives, college fairs, career days, colleges;
   - help plan summer visits, interviews, and acquisition of promotional literature;

– have students write for information about admissions and financial aid; and

– suggest discussions with students presently in college.

6. Twelfth Grade:

– Arrange for family to receive schedule of admissions testing dates and additional guidance materials, attend college planning workshops on admissions and financial aid, visit campuses;

– organise student workshops on college choice, review requirements;

– have students take tests;

– encourage students to seek counsel on college admissions, applications, and soliciting references;

– advise students to speak to college representatives;

– ensure that students complete and submit all admissions and financial aid applications before deadlines; and

– advise on replying to college responses regarding financial aid.

Role of the School Counsellor

The National Association for College Admission Counselling (NACAC) in U.S. has had a long-standing interest in meeting the educational needs of all students and improving the quality of American education. We believe that education is an investment in the future, the future of each individual student, and society at large. A strong democracy requires an educated citizenry, and we believe it is incumbent upon this nation to educate each child to his/her potential for self-fulfilment, while insuring our strength as a people able to compete in the international community.

Assisting students in reaching their full potential requires the cooperative efforts of school administrators, teachers, community representatives, government officials, parents, and the students themselves, as well as a trained staff of school counsellors who are able to facilitate student development and achievement. Of particular importance to student success is access to a strong precollege guidance and counselling programme that begins early in the student's school career. Early planning (e.g., secondary school course selection and precollege enrichment programmes) can insure that students pursue the most challenging curriculum that results in enhanced postsecondary educational options.

The vast array of postsecondary opportunities and the attendant requirements for access, coupled with rising college costs and the complexity of the financial aid system, call for a guidance support system to assist students and their parents. Critical to the success of such a support system is the strength of the articulation process between the school counsellor and college admission personnel. When the role of each is understood by the other and when communication between them has been effective, counsellors and admission personnel are in a position to help students and parents by providing accurate, up-to-date information which will assist them in making sound educational decisions. Demographic surveys indicate that our student population is changing.

Our schools are now enrolling larger numbers of students from diverse ethnic/racial backgrounds. These students are less likely to come from families with role models who have experienced or had access to postsecondary opportunities and, as a result, there will be greater reliance on the school system to provide appropriate precollege guidance and counselling experiences. In recent years, The College Board Commission on Precollege Guidance and Counselling, the NACAC sponsored National College Counselling Project, and the Carnegie Foundation for the Advancement of Teaching report on secondary education in America, have each called for the improvement and extension of precollege guidance and counselling programmes that assist students as they consider and plan for a full range of postsecondary opportunities.

NACAC believes that precollege guidance and counselling represents a developmental process that must begin at the middle or junior high school level. Such a programme takes into account that students have different needs at various educational levels and counsellors must intervene as necessary with the delivery of services and activities appropriate to each level. We have observed that counsellors have often been less involved with precollege guidance and counselling concerns because counselling time and energy have been directed toward a myriad of personal, social, and mental health concerns that could be more effectively addressed if shared with other school and community agencies. An effective guidance and counselling programme should include the following components at all levels:

- A written statement of philosophy that is consistent with the school's overall philosophy.
- A written comprehensive plan of action that outlines student needs and sets forth goals and objectives for meeting those needs.
- An evaluation process that measures progress toward meeting stated goals and objectives.

– A focus on precollege guidance and counselling that enables students to prepare themselves academically for a wide range of educational and career opportunities.

– Differentiated staffing that includes a sufficient number of counsellors with counselling loads that enable them to accomplish programme goals and objectives, the provision of appropriate administrative and supervisory support, and support personnel adequate to meet programme needs. First, precollege guidance and counselling should be known, understood, and implemented by all counsellors. Further, we see benefit in identifying counsellors who specialise in precollege guidance and counselling as distinct from other counsellors who are concerned with a wider range of student needs.

– Effective communication with a variety of constituencies, including students, parents, all educators, and the larger community.

– Counsellors and other educators committed to the principles of equal opportunity and affirmative action. This assumes the presence of positive attitudes that promote student development regardless of race, sex, or disability, and encourages the inclusion of role models among the staff who reflect these characteristics.

– A supportive instructional and administrative staff who work cooperatively with counsellors to assist students in achieving educational goals consistent with their aptitudes, abilities, and interests.

– An environment that recognises each person's worth in a complex multicultural, changing society, one that supports and encourages each student to reach his/her potential.

– Respect for student privacy and the need for confidentiality of records.

– Delivery of services according to ethical practices developed by NACAC and other similar education groups.

– Assurance to students and parents that counselling professionals have been properly trained to carry out the precollege guidance and counselling responsibilities. Further provisions should be made for release time and financial support for counsellors to attend professional meetings, workshops, and other professional development activities where they can learn skills, exchange ideas, network with other professionals, and keep up-to-date on changes in the college admission and financial aid processes.

– Adequate facilities, resources, and equipment to accomplish the goals of the programme.

Responsibilities of the School Counsellor in Precollege Guidance and Counselling

An effective precollege guidance and counselling component in a school guidance programme will insure that certain functions are performed by school counsellors. These include:

Middle or Junior High School Level

The role of the counsellor in precollege guidance and counselling at the middle or junior high school level is to:

- Implement the goals and objectives of the counselling programme by serving students, parents, and staff.
- Assist students in the development of effective study skills and learning habits that promote academic excellence.
- Promote the development of student self-awareness including an understanding of their individual abilities, interests, values, and personal attitudes.
- Guide students in their awareness and planning of their secondary school curriculum, including the selection of a course of study that will enable them to maximise their educational and career options.
- Assist students and parents in understanding the techniques and strategies of educational exploration in the college admission process.
- Broaden student's horizons by introducing them to the variety of postsecondary educational opportunities available and the educational routes to each.
- Assist students and parents in understanding the role of testing in education and the individual interpretation of all standardised test results.
- Assist students in the development of career awareness, exploration, and life-planning skills.
- Assist parents in understanding the cost of postsecondary education, the need for financial planning, and the financial aid process.

Secondary School Level

The role of the counsellor in precollege guidance and counselling at various stages of the secondary school level is, first, to continue all appropriate middle/junior high school functions to insure comprehensiveness and articulation and, in addition, to:

- Meet with students and parents regularly to review academic progress and select appropriate courses.
- Assist students in relating their abilities, aptitudes, and interests to current and future educational and occupational choices.
- Assist students in setting realistic goals, developing decision-making skills, and accepting responsibility for the decisions they make.
- Address special needs of underrepresented students, (e.g., minority students, women, students with disabilities, economically disadvantaged students, or other populations) by keeping up-to-date on programmes and resources designed specifically for these students and insuring that the students are aware of them.
- Assist students and parents in understanding the college admission and financial aid processes by providing access to current, clear, and concise information concerning the wide range of postsecondary educational opportunities available, entrance requirements, financial aid, curricular offering, costs, admission and financial aid deadlines, and the variety of early admission and early decision programmes available.
- Assist students in the acquisition, evaluation, and appropriate use of information, including college guidebooks and catalogues, computer-based guidance systems, and college videos.

- Encourage student and parent participation in college fair programmes, admission and financial aid workshops, and related programmes.
- Assist students in selecting and registering for appropriate college admission tests, and in interpreting resulting test scores and their influence in the admission process.
- Assist students with developing a personal timeline or calendar for completing the tasks associated with the college admission process.
- Work with students and teachers in developing students' essay-writing skills.
- Encourage students to visit college campuses, if possible, to gain first-hand information from admission and financial aid representatives, observe classes, and interact with faculty and students.
- Assist students in developing appropriate interviewing skills and in understanding the purpose of the college admission interview and their role in the process.
- Encourage student participation in on-campus precollege enrichment programmes.
- Develop productive relationships with colleges to assist them in understanding the nature of the school curriculum and the quality of their students' preparation.
- Develop and disseminate a school profile for use by colleges and universities.
- Work with college admission representatives to schedule visits to the school so that students will have opportunities to explore a variety of options.

- Advocate on behalf of students via letters of recommendation and personal communication with college representatives.
- Work with the school instructional staff in understanding their role in supporting students as they make important educational and career choices.
- Provide a supportive environment for students and parents and work to eliminate or reduce unnecessary anxiety too often associated with the college admission process.
- Assist students in dealing with difficult situations such as college admission and/or financial aid denials and in developing alternative strategies should this occur.
- Assist students and parents with preparation for the separation process that will occur in the school to college transition.

5

Counselling for Second Language Learners

Strategy training aims to provide learners with the tools to do the following:

- Self-diagnose their strengths and weaknesses in language learning
- Become aware of what helps them to learn the target language most efficiently
- Develop a broad range of problem-solving skills
- Experiment with familiar and unfamiliar learning strategies
- Make decisions about how to approach a language task
- Monitor and self-evaluate their performance
- Transfer successful strategies to new learning contexts.

Strategies can be categorised as either language learning or language use strategies. Language learning strategies are conscious thoughts and behaviours used by learners with the explicit goal of improving their knowledge and understanding of a target language. They include cognitive strategies for memorising and manipulating target language structures, metacognitive strategies for managing and supervising strategy use, affective strategies for gauging emotional reactions to learning and for lowering anxieties, and social strategies for enhancing learning, such as cooperating with other learners and seeking to interact with native speakers.

Language use strategies come into play once the language material is already accessible, even in some preliminary form. Their focus is to help students utilise the language they have already learned. Language use strategies include strategies for retrieving information about the language already stored in memory, rehearsing target language structures, and communicating in the language despite gaps in target language knowledge. Although no empirical evidence has yet been provided to determine a single best method for conducting strategy training, at least three different instructional frameworks have been identified.

Each has been designed to raise student awareness of the purpose and rationale of strategy use, give students opportunities to practice the strategies they are being taught, and help them use the strategies in new learning contexts.

One framework, proposed by Pearson and Dole with reference to first language learning but applicable to the study of a second language as well, targets isolated strategies by including explicit modelling and explanation of the benefits of applying a specific strategy, extensive functional practice with the strategy, and an opportunity to transfer the strategy to new learning contexts. The sequence includes the following steps:

— Initial modelling of the strategy by the teacher, with direct explanation of the strategy's use and importance
— Guided practice with the strategy

- Consolidation, where teachers help students identify the strategy and decide when it might be used
- Independent practice with the strategy
- Application of the strategy to new tasks

In the second framework, Oxford et al. outline a useful sequence for the introduction of strategies that emphasises explicit strategy awareness, discussion of the benefits of strategy use, functional and contextualised practice with the strategies, self-evaluation and monitoring of language performance, and suggestions for or demonstrations of the transferability of the strategies to new tasks. This sequence is not prescriptive of strategies that the learners are supposed to use, but rather descriptive of the various strategies that they could use for a broad range of learning tasks.

The third framework, developed by Chamot and O'Malley, is especially useful after students have already had practice in applying a broad range of strategies in a variety of contexts. Their approach to helping students complete language learning tasks can be described as a four-stage problem-solving process.

(1) Planning. Students plan ways to approach a learning task.

(2) Monitoring. Students self-monitor their performance by paying attention to their strategy use and checking comprehension.

(3) Problem Solving. Students find solutions to problems they encounter.

(4) Evaluation. Students learn to evaluate the effectiveness of a given strategy after it has been applied to a learning task.

A variety of instructional models for foreign language strategy training have already been developed and implemented in a variety of educational settings. Seven of these are described below.

General Study Skills Courses

These courses are sometimes intended for students with academic difficulties but can also target successful students who want to improve their study habits. Many general academic skills can be transferred to the process of learning a foreign language, such as using flash cards, overcoming anxiety, and learning good note-taking skills. These courses sometimes include language learning as a specific topic to highlight how learning a foreign language may differ from learning other academic subjects. Foreign language students can be encouraged to participate in order to develop general learning strategies.

Awareness Training

Also known as consciousness-raising or familiarisation training, this consists most often of isolated lectures and discussions and is usually separate from regular classroom instruction. This approach provides students with a general introduction to strategy applications. Oxford describes awareness training as "a programme in which participants become aware of and familiar with the general idea of language learning strategies and the way such strategies can help them accomplish various language tasks".

Strategy Workshops: Short workshops are another, usually more intensive, approach to increasing learner awareness of strategies through various consciousness-raising and strategy-assessment activities. They may help to improve specific language skills or present ideas for learning certain aspects of a particular foreign language. These workshops may be offered as non-credit courses or required as part of a language or academic skills course. They often combine lectures, hands-on practice with specific strategies, and discussions about the effectiveness of strategy use.

Peer Tutoring: "Tandem" or peer tutoring programmes began in the 1970s in Europe and are flourishing in many universities across the United States. Holec describes this system as "a direct language exchange" programme that pairs students of different native language backgrounds for mutual tutoring sessions (e.g., an English-speaking student studying Italian and a native-Italian-speaking student learning English). Requirements of the tutoring sessions are that students have regular meetings, alternate roles of learner and teacher, practice the two languages separately, and devote equal amounts of time to each language. Often, students exchange suggestions about the language learning strategies they use, thus providing an ad hoc form of strategy training.

Another approach to peer sessions is to encourage students who are studying the same language to organise regular target-language study groups. Students who have already completed the language course may also be invited to these meetings. Less proficient students can benefit from the language skills of more proficient students, and more proficient students may yield better insights into the particular difficulties of the target language than a teacher.

Strategies in Language Textbooks: Many foreign language textbooks have begun to embed strategies into their curricula. However, unless the strategies are explained, modeled, or reinforced by the classroom teacher, students may not be aware that they are using strategies at all. A few language textbooks provide strategy-embedded activities and explicit explanations of the benefits and applications of the strategies they address. Because the focus of the activities is contextualised language learning, learners can develop their learning strategy repertoires while learning the target language. One advantage of using textbooks with explicit strategy training is that students do not need extracurricular training; the textbooks reinforce strategy use across both tasks and skills, encouraging students to continue applying them on their own.

Videotaped Mini-Courses: Rubin developed an interactive videodisc programme and accompanying instructional guide aimed at raising students' awareness of learning strategies and of the learning process in general, to show students how to transfer strategies to new tasks and to help them take charge of their own progress while learning the language. Using authentic language situations, the instructional programme includes 20 foreign languages and offers the opportunity to select the language, topic, and difficulty level. Materials are structured to expose students to various strategies for use in many different contexts.

Strategies-Based Instruction (SBI): SBI is a learner-centered approach to teaching that extends classroom strategy training to include both implicit and explicit integration of strategies into the course content. Students experience the advantages of systematically applying the strategies to the learning and use of the language they are studying. In addition, they have opportunities to share their preferred strategies with other students and to increase their strategy use in the typical language tasks they are asked to perform. Teachers can individualise strategy training, suggest language-specific strategies, and reinforce strategies while presenting the regular course content. In a typical SBI classroom, teachers do the following:

- Describe, model, and give examples of potentially useful strategies
- Elicit additional examples from students, based on students' own learning experiences
- Lead small-group and whole-class discussions about strategies
- Encourage students to experiment with a broad range of strategies
- Integrate strategies into everyday class materials, explicitly and implicitly embedding them into the language tasks to provide for contextualised strategy practice.

Teachers may conduct SBI instruction by starting with established course materials, then determining which strategies to insert and where; starting with a set of strategies they wish to focus on and design activities around them; or inserting strategies spontaneously into the lessons whenever it seems appropriate (e.g., to help students overcome problems with difficult material or to speed up the lesson).

Designing of Strategy Training

The approaches outlined above offer options for providing strategy training to a large number of learners. Based on the needs, resources, and time available to an institution, the next step is to plan the instruction students will receive. The following seven steps are based largely on suggestions of strategy trainingby Oxford. The model is especially useful because it can be adapted to the needs of various groups of learners, the resources available, and the length of the strategy training.

1. Determine learners' needs and the resources available for training.
2. Select the strategies to be taught.
3. Consider the benefits of integrated strategy training.
4. Consider motivational issues.
5. Prepare the materials and activities.
6. Conduct explicit strategy training.
7. Evaluate and revise the strategy training.

6

School Guidance Programmes

To achieve accountability, evaluation is needed concerning the nature, structure, organisation and implementation of school district/building guidance programmes; the school counsellors and other personnel who are implementing the programmes; and the impact the programmes are having on students, the schools where they learn, and the communities in which they live. Thus, the overall evaluation of school district/building guidance programmes needs to be approached from three perspectives: programme evaluation, personnel evaluation, and results evaluation.

Guidance programme evaluation asks two questions. First, is there a written guidance programme in the school district? And second, is the written guidance programme the actual implemented programme in the buildings of the district? Discrepancies between the written programme and the implemented programme, if present, will come into sharp focus as the programme evaluation process unfolds. To conduct programme evaluation, programme standards are required. Programme standards are acknowledged measures of comparison or the criteria used to make judgments about the adequacy of the nature and structure of the programme as well as the degree to which the programme is in place.

To make judgments about guidance programmes using standards, evidence is needed concerning whether or not the standards are being met. In programme evaluation such evidence is called documentation. Using the standard listed above, evidence that the standard is in place might include the following:

1. A developmentally appropriate guidance curriculum that teaches all students the knowledge and skills they need to be self-sufficient and lead socially responsible lives.

2. Yearly schedule that incorporates the classroom guidance plan.

Documentation of such evidence could include:

1. guidance curriculum guides
2. teachers' and counsellors' unit and lesson plans
3. yearly master calendar for the guidance programme
4. curriculum materials

Sometimes the programme evaluation process is called a programme audit. The American School Counsellor Association, for example, uses the "term" audit in its programme evaluation materials. The Association has developed guidelines for a programme audit for secondary schools, for middle/junior high schools, and for elementary schools.

Personnel Evaluation

Personnel evaluation begins with the organisational structure and activities of the guidance programme in a school district. A major first step is the development of job descriptions that are based directly on the structure and activities of a school district's guidance programme.

Using the Missouri Comprehensive Guidance Programme framework for example, the job description of a school counsellor would include the following key duties: implementing the guidance curriculum; counselling individuals and small groups concerning their educational and occupational plans; counselling individuals and small groups with immediate needs and specific problems; consulting with parents and teachers; referring students to appropriate community agencies; coordinating, conducting, and being involved with activities that improve the operation of the school; evaluating and updating the guidance programme; and continuing professional development.

Guidance programme personnel evaluation is based directly on their job task descriptions and usually has two parts: a formative part (supervision) and a summative part (evaluation). The job task description identifies the performance areas to be supervised and evaluated. Gysbers and Henderson have developed an extensive listing of job task descriptors for school counsellors grouped under the basic guidance programme components of guidance curriculum, individual planning, responsive services, and system support plus the areas of professional relationships and professional responsibilities.

Having established that a guidance programme is operating in a school district through programme evaluation, and having established through personnel evaluation that school counsellors and other guidance programme personnel are carrying out the duties listed on their job descriptions 100% of the time, it now is possible to evaluate the results of the programme. Johnson suggested that there are long-range, intermediate, immediate, and unplanned-for results that need consideration. According to Johnson, long-range results focus on how programmes affect students after they have left school.

Usually long-range results are gathered using follow-up studies. Intermediate results focus on the knowledge and skills all students may gain by graduation from participating in the guidance programme. Immediate results are the knowledge and skills students may gain from participating in specific guidance activities. Finally, the possibility of unplanned-for results that may occur as a consequence of guidance activities conducted as a part of the guidance programme also need to be taken into account.

Immediate Evaluation

Do students master guidance competencies? Johnson outlined the following procedures to answer this question for immediate results. First the competencies to be mastered need to be identified. Second what results (what students should be able to write, what they may be able to talk about, or what they may be able to do) are specified. Then who will conduct the evaluation is decided. This is followed by when the evaluation is done. Then criteria are established so that judgments can be made about students' mastery of guidance competencies. Finally, how all of this is done is specified.

Do students master guidance competencies? Another way to conduct immediate evaluation, to measure mastery of guidance competencies, is the use of a confidence survey. In this format, guidance competencies are listed and students are asked to rate how confident they are that they have mastered these competencies. The confidence survey can then be used as a pre-post measure. Gain scores can be obtained and related to such measures as academic achievement and vocational identity.

INTERMEDIATE EVALUATION

Do students develop and use career plans? In making judgments concerning the career plans of students, criteria need to be identified as to what makes good plans. Four criteria are recommended; plans need to be comprehensive, developmental, student-centered and student-directed, and competency based. Based on these criteria, one way to evaluate students' career plans is to judge the extent to which the activities included in the Individual Planning Component of the guidance programme lead to the development of plans that meet these criteria. A second way is to make judgments about the adequacy of the plan contents. Finally, a third way is to judge their use. Do students actually use their career plans in planning for the future?

7

Counselling for Gifted Students

The concept of an underachieving gifted student may seem inherently contradictory if intellectually gifted students are seen only as those who excel in school at high levels of academic achievement. However, since the new federal definition was formulated in the early 1970s, there has been growing support in the field for defining intellectual giftedness as exceptional potential for high academic achievement, whether or not it has been demonstrated at school. it is assumed that the gifted underachiever has exceptional potential. A student may be gifted in one or many areas of learning or cognitive processing; however, few mentally gifted students have the capability of truly excelling in all subjects and on all kinds of academic tasks.

Gifted underachievers manifest three patterns of behavioural responses to the school setting:

(a) non-communicative and withdrawn,

(b) passively complying to "get by," and

(c) aggressive/disruptive "problem" students.

Behaviour patterns of all three groups tend to reflect feelings of low self-esteem, a lack of belief in their ability to influence outcomes in school, an unrealistic self-concept, and negative attitudes toward school. Generally, these students tend to be loners who have difficulty making or maintaining friendships.

Increasing numbers of intellectually gifted students who have not been recognised and served as gifted because of relatively low patterns of achievement have been discovered over the last two decades as a result of three significant changes in educational practices. First, there has been an increase in the use of tests and sophisticated assessment procedures. Second, there has been an increase in teacher referrals for special education services because of learning or behavioural problems. Third, there has been an increased effort to recognise and develop the potential abilities of culturally different and minority children.

Gifted underachievers are also identified as a result of parental accounts of out-of-school behaviours that show advanced interests and skills. The most disconcerting group of gifted underachievers are those who are not recognised while in school. Awareness of this group has developed primarily through the identification of adults with superior intellectual abilities whose school records show mediocre or poor academic performance.

Identification of Gifted Underachievers

The first reason is obvious—the loss of potential contributions to society from that individual. The second reason is not so obvious—the underachiever's vulnerability to significant mental health and social problems. Often the gifted underachiever becomes a disturbing behavioural problem both at home and at school. This problem is a natural consequence of the conflict between the individual's personal psychological needs and the lack of opportunities for appropriate learning provided by the school. The third reason is that early identification permits a better chance for reversing patterns of underachievement.

Causes of Underachievement

- Lack of motivation. Many highly gifted and creative children have learning styles that are incompatible with prevailing instructional methods. Furthermore, the level of instruction may be inappropriate for these students and the restrictions on learning in the classroom discourage their full participation.
- Values Conflict. Students may not want to participate in school because of conflicts between the values of the school or the gifted programme and the values held by the individuals and/or the cultures from which they come; for example, female students from cultures in which a college education or a career is not expected may underachieve.
- Lack of environmental nurturance of intelluctual potential. Low socioeconomic status families often fail to provide exposure that stimulates the development of higher level thinking skills. Enriching experiences such as travel, educational activities, and shared problem solving may be neglected. Such students may be from isolated rural settings, economically disadvantaged urban sites, or specific ethnic or cultural minorities that do not encourage intellectual development.
- Developmental delays or chronic poor health. These students are characterised by relatively low energy levels or interfering hyperactivity. They may have a mild delay in perceptual motor skill development, or

a general immaturity in all areas. Often these students have entered school as the youngest in their class.

– Specific disabilities. Impairment due to specific learning disabilities, brain damage/cerebral dysfunction or neurological impairment, or lack of normal hearing or visual perception may be the cause of underachievement. Some of these students are in fact dyslexic or neurologically disabled. It is not the disability that produces that underachievement but the lack of appropriate programming. These students frequently are not adequately challenged or encouraged to develop their intellectual abilities because of low expectations and a narrow curriculum.

– Specific or general academic skill conflicts. These students may have difficulty with writing, reading, math, or higher level skills necessary for subject matter mastery and high achievement.

Successful approaches to reversing patterns of underachievement have been based on a view that the problem behaviour has been shaped by forces within the school experience that can be altered. These forces essentially are:

(a) the social messages conveyed by the teacher and peers that invite or discourage the student to participate and

(b) the degree to which the curriculum and instruction is appropriate for the learning style and performance level of the student. Successful interventions create positive forces to shape achievement behaviour.

Programming for gifted underachievers must address three critical areas:

(a) an understanding of self – the nature of and problems related to being gifted;

(b) development of constructive ways of coping with the inevitable conflict and frustration created by the significant gap between cognitive ability and performance level; and

(c) development of a healthier, more realistic self-concept and higher self-esteem.

Effective programming for reversing patterns of underachievement can occur in self-contained classrooms, in resource rooms that provide supplementary services, or through the development of an individual educational plan that may involve a mentor in the school or community. Regardless of the structure, there are five programming components that need to be addressed:

1. The teacher(s) must accept the fact that the student is intellectually gifted, does not want to underachieve or fail, has low self-esteem, and needs to develop constructive coping skills and self-understanding. The teacher(s) must be skilled in guidance techniques, accurate in understanding the nature of giftedness, and positive in emotional response to the challenge of working with this type of student.

2. The curriculum must be challenging, personally meaningful, and rewarding to the gifted underachiever. There must be a balance between basic skill development and more advanced exploration through the arts and sciences. Career exploration and the development of personal interests are also critical motivating elements, and all learning experiences should be designed for maximum challenge and success.

3. The instruction must require minimal memorisation and drill/practice activity and provide maximal opportunity for inquiry, scientific investigation, and

creative production. Self-directed learning activities should be encouraged and the students' self-discipline nurtured. The climate created by the instructional style of the teacher should be one of excitement, anticipation, personal satisfaction, and low pressure.

4. The peer group must include at least a few other gifted students, possibly other underachievers, who may become special friends. The group must be accepting of diversity and individual differences.

5. Special services should be provided as needed for handicapped students, for those in need of remedial instruction, or for group counselling. Supplementary psychological and medical services, including family counselling, may also be needed.

Stress Management

Many gifted youngsters have a heightened sensitivity to their surroundings, to events, to ideas, and to expectations. Some experience their own high expectations for achievement as a relentless pressure to excel. Constant striving to live up to self-expectations—or those of others—to be first, best, or both can be very stressful. With every new course, new teacher, or new school, questions arise about achievement and performance, since every new situation carries with it the frightening risk of being mediocre.

Striving becomes even more stressful when unrealistic or unclear expectations are imposed by adults or peers. The pressure to excel, accompanied by other concerns such as feeling different, self-doubt (the "imposter" syndrome), and the need to prove their giftedness can drain the energy of gifted students and result in additional stress. Stress occurs even when everything is going well. Youngsters get tired from their constant efforts and may secretly fear that next time they will not be as successful.

Many gifted students accept responsibility for a variety of activities such as a demanding courseload; leadership in school activities, clubs, or sports; and part-time jobs. Even if it were humanly possible, doing everything well would be physically and emotionally stressful. Vacations may be stressful if students are comfortable only when achieving and succeeding. Taking time off may make them feel nervous and lacking control.

Gifted students need intellectual challenge. Boring, monotonous busy-work is very stressful for individuals who prefer thinking and reasoning activities. Boredom may result in anger, resentment, or, in some cases, setting personal goals for achievement and success that significantly exceed those of parents or school. Some gifted students value independence and leadership, yet the separation they feel from their peers results in loneliness and fewer opportunities to relieve stress. Finding a peer group can be difficult, particularly for adolescents. Some experience a conflict between belonging to a group and using their extraordinary abilities.

Gifted students are complex thinkers, persuasively able to argue both sides of any question. This ability, however, may complicate decisions. Students may lack information about and experience with resources, processes, outcomes, or priorities that help tip an argument toward a clear solution. Furthermore, not every problem has one obviously correct answer. Compromise and accommodation are realities in the adult world, but they are not easily perceived from a young person's viewpoint. Thus, decision making may be a very stressful process.

During the early years, school may be easy, with minimum effort required for success. If students are not challenged, they conclude that "giftedness" means instant learning, comprehension, and mastery, and that outstanding achievement follows naturally. As years pass, however, schoolwork becomes more difficult. Some students discover that they must work harder to earn top grades and that they have not developed productive study habits.

Many suspect they are no longer gifted, and their sense of self-worth is undermined. Stress can hamper the very abilities that make these students gifted. Stress clouds thinking, reduces concentration, and impairs decision making. It leads to forgetfulness and a loss of ability to focus keenly on a task, and it makes students overly sensitive to criticism. Under these conditions, they perform less well and are more upset by their failures.

Abundant gifts and the potential for success in many different subjects and careers may increase opportunities and lead to complex choices. Limiting options is a confusing and upsetting process because it means saying "no" to some attractive alternatives. A person cannot prepare to become an architect and a financial planner, or an advertising executive and a scientist. At some point, the education needed for one career splits from that needed for the other. To set career goals, students must know themselves well as individuals. They must understand their own personalities, values, and goals and use self-awareness as a guide for making decisions. These activities are all stressful. Some ways of coping with stress are healthy; others are not. Some healthy ways of handling stress include the following:

- Change the source of the stress. Do something else for a while. Put down those study notes and jog for an hour.

– Confront the source of the stress. If it is a person, persuade him or her to remove the stress. Ask the teacher for an extension on a project. Sit down with the person driving you crazy and talk about ways you might better work together.

– Talk about the source of stress. Rid yourself of frustration. Find a good listener and complain. Talk through possible solutions.

– Shift your perspective. Tell yourself that each new situation or problem is a new challenge, and that there is something to be learned from every experience.

Learn skills and attitudes that make tasks easier and more successful. Practice effective organisation and time-management skills. For example, large projects are easier and less overwhelming when broken down into manageable steps. Learn to type and revise assignments on a word processor. Learn about yourself and your priorities, and use the information to make decisions. Learn how to say "no" gracefully when someone offers you another attractive (or unpleasant) task about which you have a choice. Tell yourself that this unpleasantness will be over soon and that the whole process will bring you closer to reaching your goal. Mark the days that are left on the calendar, and enjoy crossing out each one as you near the finish.

Take time out for enjoyable activities. Everyone needs a support system. Find friends, teachers, or relatives with whom you have fun. Spend time with these people when you can be yourself and set aside the pressures of school, work, or difficult relationships. As a reward for your efforts, give yourself work breaks. Listen to your favourite music, shoot baskets, or participate in some other brief activity that is mentally restful or fun.

Ignore the source of the stress. Practice a little healthy procrastination and put a pleasant activity ahead of the stressful one. This, is, of course, only a short-term solution. Get regular physical exercise and practice sound nutrition. Physical activity not only provides time out, but also changes your body chemistry as you burn off muscle tension built up from accommodating stress. Exercise also increases resistance to illness.

Nutritious food and regular meals help regulate your body chemistry and keep you functioning at your sharpest. Eating healthy and attractively prepared food can be an enjoyable activity on its own. The following are some unhealthy ways students cope with stress:

- Escaping through alcohol, drugs, frequent illness, sleep, overeating, or starving themselves. These strategies suggest a permanent withdrawal or avoidance rather than a time out.
- Selecting strategies to avoid failure. Gifted students closely link their identities to excellence and achievement. Failure, or even the perception of failure, seriously threatens their self-esteem. By not trying, or by selecting impossible goals, students can escape having their giftedness questioned. Only their lack of effort will be questioned.
- Aiming too low. This reduces stress by eliminating intense pressure or possible feelings of failure. Dogged procrastination in starting projects, selecting less competitive colleges or less rigorous courses, or dropping out of school rather than bringing home poor grades allows students to avoid feelings of failure in the short run. Sadly, this sets the stage for long-term disappointment caused by a destructive coping style.

- Overscheduling daily life with schoolwork and extracurricular activities, selecting impossibly demanding courseloads, or fussing endlessly over assignments in vain attempts to make them perfect. With this strategy, it is possible to succeed only through superhuman effort; thus the student can save face by setting goals too high for anyone to achieve.

Not all gifted youngsters are stressed by the same events. Individual responses to stress also differ. Younger students do not tend to respond to stress in the same way that teenagers do. Since each student is unique, parents and teachers will have to watch carefully to know whether a child is stressed to the point of constructive excitement or to the point of damaging overload. The following checklist includes many, but not all, symptoms of burnout:

- Student is no longer happy or pleasantly excited about school activities, but, rather, is negative or cynical toward work, teachers, classmates, parents, and the whole school- and achievement-centered experience.
- Student approaches most school assignments with resignation or resentment.
- Student exhibits boredom.
- Student suffers from sleeplessness, problems in falling asleep, or periodic waking.
- Student overreacts to normal concerns or events.
- Student experiences fatigue, extreme tiredness, low energy level.
- Student exhibits unhappiness with self and accomplishments.
- Student has nervous habits such as eye blinking, head shaking, or stuttering.

- Student has physical ailments such as weekly or daily stomachaches or headaches.
- Student is frequently ill.
- Student exhibits dependency through increased clinging or needing and demanding constant support and reassurance.
- Student engages in attention-getting behaviours such as aggressive or acting-out behaviours.
- Student has a sense of being trapped or a feeling or being out of control.
- Student is unable to make decisions.
- Student has lost perspective and sense of humour.
- Student experiences increased feelings of physical, emotional, and mental exhaustion in work and activities that used to give pleasure.

Role of Parents, Teachers and Counsellors for Stress Reduction

Help each gifted student understand and cope with his or her intellectual, social, and emotional needs during each stage of development. In some ways, the needs of gifted students mirror those of more typical children. Giftedness, however, adds a special dimension to self-understanding and self-acceptance. If gifted youngsters are to develop into self-fulfilled adults, the following differential needs must be addressed:

(a) the need to understand the ways in which they are different from others and the ways in which they are the same;

(b) the need to accept their abilities, talents, and limitations;

(c) the need to develop social skills;

(d) the need to feel understood and accepted by others; and

(e) the need to develop an understanding of the distinction between "pursuit of excellence" and "pursuit of perfection."

Help each gifted student develop a realistic and accurate self-concept. Giftedness does not mean instant mastery or winning awards. Parents and teachers need to set realistic expectations for efforts and achievements and help the student choose appropriate goals. It is important to recognise and appreciate efforts and improvement. On the other hand, giftedness permits people to learn and use information in unusual ways.

Given parental support and encouragement, personal motivation, and opportunities to learn and apply their knowledge, gifted students may enjoy the process of creating new ideas, especially if they believe that it is all right to think differently than age-mates. Help each gifted student be a whole person. Gifted youngsters are children first and gifted second. While their learning styles may be special, they are individuals with emotions, likes and dislikes, and unique personalities. They will not wake up one day and be "not gifted." They should not feel responsible for solving world problems, nor does the world owe them tribute. It is up to each student to make life meaningful. Understanding these realistic limits to the bounty of giftedness can reduce stress on confused students. Gifted students have strong emotions that give personal meaning to each experience. Emotions should be recognised, understood, and used as a valid basis for appropriate behaviours.

Show patience. Let students select and strive toward their own goals. Do not compare them or their achievements to others. Some gifted students are intensely curious and may have less tolerance for ambiguity and unpredictability than their age-mates. Help them develop patience with themselves.

Show acceptance and encouragement. Encourage students to work purposefully, thoughtfully, and thoroughly and do the best they can. It is not necessary to excel in every situation. Help them develop priorities to decide which tasks require the best efforts and which require simply "good enough." Accept and reward efforts and the process of working on tasks. Sincere effort is valuable in itself and deserves reinforcement. The means may be more deserving of merit than the ends.

Efforts are within the gifted students' control; the outcomes (high grades, prizes, honors, etc.) are not. Show love and acceptance, regardless of the outcome. These youngsters need to be cherished as individuals, not simply for their accomplishments. They must know that they can go home and be loved—and continue to love themselves—even when they do not finish first or best. Encourage flexibility and appropriate behaviour. Curiosity is frequently mentioned as a characteristic of gifted learners.

Many individuals agree that gifted students seem to question rules automatically, asking "How come?" Concerned adults can reduce stress on gifted students by helping them distinguish between hard-and-fast rules that should be followed and those that can safely be questioned or altered and helping them understand why rules sometimes change from time to time. Many people recognise that new ideas come from reshaping and discarding old notions of right and wrong and want students to be inquiring, creative, and resourceful thinkers. But society, schools, teachers, and academic subjects have rules.

In our society, flagrant rule breakers may be penalised and shut out of opportunities for further growth and enrichment. Our students will become better thinkers by learning that rules are man-made guides to behaviour, not perfect or divine, but they are to be learned, understood, and followed appropriately in certain situations. For instance, not every student will like every teacher, but showing respect is appropriate behaviour even if the student privately thinks otherwise. Wise adults can model problem-solving methods that result in workable solutions and help gifted students learn when and how to use their novel perceptions, creativity, and independent thoughts appropriately and effectively.

Understanding and following rules does not mean conforming to every situation. There are some occasions when gifted students should not be expected to accommodate others. For example, a severe mismatch between a youngster's ability level and a school programme may be very stressful. Altering the student's curriculum may solve the problem. Some parents unintentionally send mixed messages regarding behaviour. When children are rude or uncooperative and offend teachers, other adults, or peers, their parents behave as though giftedness somehow excuses such behaviour and the offending actions highlight their child's specialness. Some even seem pleased.

These parents do their children a great disservice by denying them the opportunity to learn empathy, teamwork, and tolerance for individual differences. Let students live their own lives. Caring adults support, encourage, and celebrate students' efforts and successes, but they stand back a bit from these efforts and achievements. They let students select and master activities for personal enjoyment. Unfortunately, some students wonder whether their efforts and gains are for personal satisfaction or to please overly involved parents, teachers, or others. When these students wish to give up an activity that no longer brings pleasure or interest, they fear they will disappoint others, and they are likely to feel trapped.

Be available for guidance and advice. Some gifted students appear to be more mature than their chronological age indicates. They have advanced verbal skills and can talk a good line. Nevertheless, they are still children and need realistic, clearly stated guidelines about limits, values, and proper behaviour. These young people may not have enough information or experience to make wise and effective decisions. They may not understand decision-making processes, and they need wise adults to listen and guide as they talk through the problem, the alternatives, and the pro's and con's and try out choices.

Knowing that they can be independent and still talk through their thoughts with others without losing face reduces stress for these students. Gifted students need to hear adults openly state some of their perspectives to understand expectations and acceptable limits. While these students are very perceptive, they cannot read minds. Gifted students may know more facts about their interest area than do their parents and other adults. However, they have not lived longer; they need loving concern and guidance.

Gifted Children with Attention Deficit Hyperactivity Disorder (ADHD)

Gifted children whose attention deficits are identified later may be at risk for developing learned helplessness and chronic underachievement. ADHD children whose giftedness goes unrecognised do not receive appropriate educational services. It is recommended that children who fail to meet test score criteria for giftedness and are later diagnosed with ADHD be retested for the gifted programme. As a group, ADHD children tend to lag two to three years behind their age peers in social and emotional maturity.

Gifted ADHD children are no exception. This finding has important implications for educational placement. As a group, gifted children without ADHD tend to be more similar in their cognitive, social, and emotional development to children two to four years older than children their own age. When placed with other high ability children without the disorder, ADHD children may find the advanced maturity of their classmates a challenge they are ill prepared for.

Also, gifted children without the disorder may have little patience for the social and emotional immaturity of the gifted ADHD student in their midst. This is not to say that gifted ADHD students should not be placed with other gifted students. The research is clear that lack of intellectual challenge and little access to others with similar interests, ability, and drive are often risk factors for gifted children, contributing to social or emotional problems.

It is difficult to differentiate true attention deficits from the range of temperament and behaviour common to gifted children. There is concern in the literature that clinicians err on the side of pathologising normal gifted behaviour. Common characteristics of gifted children can be misconstrued as indicators of pathology when the observer is unfamiliar with the differences in the development of gifted children. This difficulty can be exacerbated when the gifted child in question spends considerable time in a classroom where appropriate educational services are not provided.

The intensity, drive, perfectionism, curiosity, and impatience commonly seen in gifted children may, in some instances, be mistaken for indicators of ADHD. The creatively gifted child may appear to be oppositional, hyperactive, and argumentative. Gifted children with some kinds of undiagnosed learning disabilities will be very disorganised, messy, and have difficult social relations. Ideally, a diagnosis of ADHD in gifted children should be made by a multidisciplinary team that includes at least one clinician trained in differentiating childhood psychopathologies and one professional who understands the normal range of developmental characteristics of gifted children.

Since as many as two thirds of children with ADHD have coexisting conditions such as learning disabilities or depression, assessment must include an evaluation for these disorders as well. School personnel rarely have the training needed to differentially diagnose ADHD, and few clinicians are aware of the unique developmental characteristics of gifted children. Accurate assessment must be a team effort. One of the reasons parents may be hesitant to comply with treatment recommendations for their children is because they aren't convinced their child has the disorder. Parents want a thorough evaluation, and parents of gifted children want assurance that their child's giftedness has been taken into consideration when evaluations are conducted. When parents see that their child has been properly evaluated, they may be more willing to participate in a treatment plan.

Attention Deficit Disorder without Hyperactivity (ADD)

Attention Deficit Disorder without Hyperactivity (ADD) or with Hyperactivity (ADHD) continues to be a misunderstood diagnosis by many. Some parents and teachers still hold a perception that the label simply provides an excuse for disruptive behaviour; however, studies continue to support a biochemical or organic basis to the disorder. Presentation of symptoms can be affected by family interactions, school expectations, and other demands placed on the individual child. Part of the reason that attention deficit is usually diagnosed in school age children (e.g., first to third grade) is attributable to the demands placed on the child when beginning school (American Psychiatric Association [APA]).

The structure at school differs from that in the home or preschool environment. Typical predisposing factors within the individual, as well as in the family history, are being identified in the literature. For example, a history of alcoholism, smoking, or depression in parents can be predisposing factors. Certain physiological markers, such as frequent early ear infections, have also been associated with the presentation of attention deficit.

Physical complications can be a factor in the development of language and reading disabilities that are associated with attention deficit for between 45% and 60% of those diagnosed. Attention Deficit Disorder presents in a slightly different way for each individual, partially due to the factors noted above. Although there is a cluster of symptoms usually associated with the disorder, the individual presentation can be just as varied as the predisposing factors.

Diagnosis in children and adults is usually made by history, self-report, and observation from significant others in the person's life. Central to diagnosis in children are the symptoms in the general areas of inattention, impulsivity, and hyperactivity. In adults, the most prominent symptom is inattention.

Symptoms of attention deficit can be mimicked by emotional disorders, e.g., reaction to abuse, depression or anxiety. If therapy is not successful in addressing underlying emotional concerns, medication may be used with positive results just as in the case of more classic symptoms of ADHD. In those cases where early abuse or neglect has been instrumental in affecting the neurology of the individual, the actual outcome, and thus treatment, may not differ significantly from other cases of ADHD. Difficulty sleeping is often seen with attention deficit, particularly for those with hyperactivity. Sleep problems can also be exacerbated by medication use.

Other disorders may co-occur with Attention Deficit Disorder. Those commonly observed include: Tourette's, Obsessive-Compulsive Disorder, Depression, Autism, Oppositional Defiant Disorder (ODD), or Conduct Disorder (CD). The relationship between ADHD, ODD, and CD is often presented on a continuum or as a progressive relationship. Symptoms of ADHD often present initially, followed by ODD, and ultimately CD for a small percentage of those with initial attention problems. Individual characteristics, family factors, and life experiences all interact to push some individuals through this continuum to more serious behavioural concerns.

The comorbidity of other disorders or symptoms often makes successful treatment more difficult. Other features of ADHD include differences in level of executive functioning between those who present with hyperactivity and those who do not. Deficits in executive functioning are associated with greater hyperactivity and impulsivity. These differences in executive functioning include an inability to self-monitor and self-control. Prevalence estimates for ADHD and ADD are between 3 to 7% of school age children.

Treatment

Effective treatment usually combines medication and therapy, including behavioural interventions aimed at increasing structure at home and school. Parents and teachers are active participants in successful treatment efforts. Stimulants are the most commonly used medications, with some use of anti-depressants, for co-morbid conditions of depression and anxiety. Other interventions include parent training and family therapy, individual therapy, support groups, and social skills training.

Providing structure for these individuals, and helping children learn to provide structure for themselves, are at the core of successful interventions. Although medication is often part of a successful treatment approach, school personnel are usually not directly involved in recommending a prescription. Diagnoses and prescriptions can only be provided by the family physician, pediatrician, or psychiatrist. Even the process of referral can expose a school to liability for financial responsibility, so the counsellor needs to be aware of the manner in which any conversation about medication or referral takes place.

Role of Counsellor

The counsellor's role in enhancing the academic performance of students with ADD or ADHD often involves consultation with teachers around classroom interventions, as well as providing support and education to parents. In addition to basic behavioural interventions, coping skills, social skills, and self-monitoring skills are important tools that can be reviewed through various modalities, including individual counselling, group sessions, or classroom guidance modules.

Providing workshops in the evening with separate sessions for parents and children can be a resource welcomed by parents. Such efforts may be jointly offered with community support groups. Parents often need information about appropriate expectations for behaviour and school work, positive parenting techniques, and support groups at the school or in the community, such as CHADD (a support group for children and adults with attention deficit disorder). For example, a counselling newsletter to parents can provide descriptions of ADD, such as the fact that disruptive behaviours observed at school may not be observed at home, or that behaviour can be inconsistent—at times under the child's control, and impulsive at others.

Information and support can help parents in making the decision to seek an evaluation. Typical challenges for students with ADD or ADHD include:

1) organisational problems;
2) problems with transitions;
3) acting as if rules don't apply to them;
4) adopting a negative attitude out of frustration in academic tasks, social interactions, or as a defence against low self esteem;
5) experiencing isolation or exclusion from peers;
6) poor grades as a result of rushing through assignments, incomplete work, or distractibility in class;

7) impulsive behaviour;
8) difficulty sustaining attention;
9) different learning styles; or
10) disruption of sleep or appetite, as a result of ADD or medication.

These students often describe feeling bored at school, and may appear oppositional. Motivation around academic tasks or conforming to rules can be a challenge for these students. A simple intervention that has proven successful includes "chunking" or organising assignments into smaller sections. This makes successful completion a more likely outcome, and if applied to in-class assignments, allows the student a legitimate reason to get up and walk to the teacher's desk. Even such a small amount of movement can help discharge energy that is so critical for these students.

It is for this reason that a common consequence for not completing homework (i.e., losing recess) is actually counter-productive with overactive children. It is also important to remember the lack of self-monitoring ability as being central for many of these individuals. Teachers and parents can help children and adolescents develop this skill. Mechanisms to increase self-awareness include external monitoring systems such as checklists in the classroom.

Additionally, the teacher can provide verbal cues such as asking the class to, "Stop and check – where is your mind?" Or the teacher can use physical monitoring cues for particular students, e.g., a simple tap on the shoulder to help them self-monitor. These cues are general enough to ensure that students don't feel ostracised by their use.

Depression in Children

Within the past three decades, it has become evident that

mood disorders are common among children and adolescents. In children and adolescents, the most frequently diagnosed mood disorders are major depressive disorder, dysthymic disorder, and bipolar disorder. These are briefly described below.

Major Depressive Disorder: Major depressive disorder is a serious condition characterised by one or more major depressive episodes. In children and adolescents, an episode lasts an average of seven to nine months. Depressed children are sad and lose interest in activities they used to enjoy. They feel unloved, pessimistic, or even hopeless; they think that life is not worth living; and they may think about or threaten suicide. They are often irritable, which may lead to disruptive or aggressive behaviour. They may be indecisive, have problems concentrating, and lack energy or motivation. They may neglect appearance and hygiene, and their normal eating and sleeping patterns may be disturbed.

Dysthymic Disorder: Dysthymic disorder has fewer symptoms, but is more persistent. The child or adolescent is depressed for most of the day on most days, and symptoms may continue for several years, the average dysthymic period being approximately four years. Seventy percent of children and adolescents with dysthymia eventually experience an episode of major depression. When this combination of major depression and dysthymia occurs, the condition is referred to as double depression.

Bipolar Disorder: In bipolar disorder, episodes of depression alternate with episodes of mania. The depressive episode usually comes first, with the first manic features becoming evident months or even years later. Adolescents with mania feel energetic and confident; may have difficulty sleeping but do not tire; and talk a great deal, often speaking very loudly or rapidly. They may complain of racing thoughts. They may do schoolwork quickly and creatively, but in a chaotic, disorganised way. In the manic stage, they may have exaggerated or even delusional ideas about their capabilities and importance, become overconfident, and be uninhibited with others. They may engage in reckless behaviour (e.g., fast driving or unsafe sex). Sexual preoccupations are increased and may be associated with promiscuous behaviour.

Approximately two-thirds of children and adolescents with major depressive disorder also have another mental disorder, such as anxiety disorder, conduct disorder, oppositional defiant disorder, psychoactive substance abuse or dependence, or phobias. Authorities have also noted that children with medical problems often face extreme and/or chronic stress, which places them at risk for depression. Estimates of depression among youngsters with medical problems range from 7% in general medical patients to 23% in orthopedic patients.

Depression has also been linked to a variety of other medical conditions, including endocrinopathies and metabolic disorders (e.g., diabetes and hypoglycemia), viral infections (e.g., influenza, viral hepatitis, and viral pneumonia), rheumatoid arthritis, cancer, central nervous system disorders, metal intoxications, and disabling diseases of all kinds. Some of these conditions may be temporary, but some may be diagnosed as primary disabilities in youngsters with health impairments.

Depression and Suicide

A number of studies have confirmed that children and adolescents with depression are at high risk for suicidal behaviour. Because mood disorders substantially increase the risk of suicide, suicidal behaviour is a matter of serious concern for parents, educators, and clinicians who deal with the mental health problems of children and adolescents. Over 90% of children and adolescents who commit suicide have a mental disorder.

The precise causes of depression are not known. Research on adults with depression generally points to both biological and psychosocial factors, but there has been considerably less research on children and adolescents.

- *Family and genetic factors*: Between 20% and 50% of depressed children and adolescents have a family history of depression. It is not clear whether the relationship between parent and childhood depression derives from genetic factors or if depressed parents create an environment in which children are more likely to develop mental disorders.
- *Biological factors*: Biochemical and physiological correlates of depression have been studied by medical researchers, with results that generally point to a chemical imbalance in the brain as a causal factor. Most of these studies have been conducted with adults, so the findings may not apply to children and adolescents.
- *Cognitive factors*: For several decades there has been considerable interest in the relationship between a pessimistic mindset and a predisposition to depression. Pessimistic individuals generally react more passively, helplessly, and ineffectively to negative events than optimistic individuals. The specific origins of pessimistic mindset have not been established but are topics of current research interest.

Recent research has focused on the development and validation of checklists and protocols to be used by mental health professionals along with clinical interviews and medical tests. An accurate diagnosis of depression is a complex task, extremely difficult for even highly skilled physicians and other clinicians. It requires a careful examination of physical, mental, emotional, environmental, and cultural factors related to the child or adolescent, his/her family, and the environment. Teachers, counsellors, and other school personnel are not expected to diagnose depression in young people; the major roles of educators are to detect the symptoms of depression and make appropriate referrals.

Treatment

Treatment approaches for children and adolescents include psychosocial interventions (e.g., cognitive behaviour therapy) and medication, as well as traditional psychotherapy. Two forms of cognitive therapy (i.e., self-control therapy for prepubertal children and coping skills for adolescents) have been judged as probably effective. A number of medications are commonly prescribed for children and adolescents with depression, but many of these have not yet been subjected to sufficient study. Effective treatment requires intervention by both medical and mental health professionals, with support from all others who come in contact with the young person; and is therefore not within the purview of the school alone.

School Intervention

The educator's most important contribution is the provision of a positive and supportive environment, components of which include satisfaction of basic needs, caring relationships with adults, and physical and psychological security. Any inclusion in a student's programme that serves to enhance feelings of self-worth, self-control, and optimism has the potential for ameliorating feelings of depression. Aversive techniques (e. g., punishment and "get tough" approaches) should be avoided to the extent possible. Educators must use instructional strategies that are both positive and effective so that the student will achieve success and enjoy the learning process.

Examples include direct instruction with positive reinforcement, thematic instrucional units with varied levels of classroom assignments, learning strategies (e. g., mnemonic devices) and utilisation of the principles of universal design for leaning, which promote access to the general curriculum for students with learning problems. Some protective factors have been addressed in published curicula (e. g., preventing alienation, enhancing self-esteem, and learning self-control). Other interventions that have implications for school programmes (e. g., phototherapy and exercise) have been found to have value in reducing symptoms of depression in adults, but have not yet been subjected to sufficient study with children and adolescents.

Disabiled Students in Career and Technical Education

Career and technical education (CTE) can provide significant benefits to disabled students. CTE teachers need to be aware of the rights of students with disabilities and of the planning process involved in meeting their needs. In addition, CTE teachers must know what role they play both in planning and in providing instruction. CTE teachers often need background information on the details of disabilities and the accommodations required.

Research shows that students with disabilities in secondary CTE programmes were less likely to drop out and more likely to be employed, to have paid competitive jobs, and to work full time after high school. However, CTE that included only simulated work experience in classroom settings did not appear to lead to optimal employment outcomes. Students with disabilities who had paid or unpaid work experience in high school had better employment outcomes—higher wages, more hours, more continuous employment.

Furthermore, students with disabilities mainstreamed into regular CTE or academic classrooms obtained paid competitive jobs more often and felt better prepared to keep their jobs. Qualitative studies reviewed by Eisenmann imply that integration of academic and vocational curricula promoted meaningful engagement and inclusion of students with disabilities by increasing persistence, academic achievement, and postsecondary engagement.

Rights of Disabled Students

Four key federal laws define the rights of students with disabilities. Two federal civil rights laws, the Americans with Disabilities Act of 1990 and Section 504 of the Rehabilitation Act of 1973, require access for students with disabilities to all federally funded programmes and prohibit discrimination based on disability in any aspect of public education programmes. The 1998 Perkins Act requires equal access for special populations, including students with disabilities, to all vocational programmes, services, and activities and prohibits discrimination based on special population status.

The Individuals with Disabilities Education Act (IDEA), as amended in 1997, establishes the right of students with disabilities to a free appropriate public education, including special education, related services, and transition services. The Individualised Education Programme (IEP) mandated by IDEA draws on the results of a comprehensive evaluation of the student's educational needs at least once every 3 years. The IEP must identify the student's current level of educational performance; measurable goals and objectives; special education, related services, and other accommodations to be provided; and the extent of participation with nondisabled students.

The IEP must also specify how the student's progress will be measured, how parents will be informed of progress, and the extent of modification in state- and districtwide tests. Beginning at age 14, the IEP must include a statement of transition services the student will need to reach postschool goals; beginning at age 16, the IEP must include a statement of transition services to help the student prepare for leaving school. IDEA requires that six participants be involved in the IEP meeting: the student (if appropriate); a parent (and family if desired); at least one of the student's special education teachers (or related services provider, if appropriate); at least one of the student's regular education teachers; a representative of the local educational agency; and other agency personnel with knowledge or expertise to meet the student's needs.

The planning process involved in IEP development includes three steps.

- the abilities, needs, interests, and preferences of the individual student are determined.
- individual postschool goals are developed based on abilities, needs, interests, and preferences.
- instructional activities and accommodations, modifications, and supports appropriate to the student's postschool goals are identified.

A variety of individuals must work together in an effective IEP team, including special education, CTE, and academic teachers, programme support staff, guidance counsellors, and school administrators. Other personnel are included as appropriate to meet the individual student's needs—for example, speech, occupational, or physical therapists; adult service providers such as rehabilitation or independent living counsellors; and employers or postsecondary education representatives. Effective planning for activities and services that benefit students with disabilities and improve postschool outcomes involves several broad practices.

Planning should be proactive, focused on individual students, and driven by students and parents; it should involve student assessment, life skills development, and accommodations. Planned educational activities should focus on school- and work-based experiences linking high academic and workplace standards, with integrated academic and vocational curricula for employment skills and specific occupational instruction. Family involvement should be facilitated by training to increase parents' knowledge and skills in advocacy, planning, support, and legal issues.

Business, labour, and government and community agencies should be actively involved to provide resources, training sites, and mentoring for students and educators. Finally, programme policy and structure should support needed partnerships, philosophy, planning, evaluation, and human resource development.

Role of CTE Teacher

CTE teachers are only one member of the team that plans

and provides educational activities and accommodations for students with disabilities. In IEP development and transition planning, CTE teachers' role is to provide information, support, and assistance to others who lead the process. However, CTE teachers play a primary role in providing instruction through school- and work-based experiences and activities linking the two and in integrating academic and vocational instruction; in that role, CTE teachers should receive support and assistance from others.

Special educators typically play the primary role in identifying educational activities and accommodations that suit students' interests, aptitudes, abilities, and postschool preferences. Trained vocational assessors, if available, may use formal assessment tools, or special educators can conduct informal assessments using data in school records; interviews with students, families, and previous instructors; or published interest, aptitude, or skills instruments.

CTE teachers may be able to provide programme inventories or assessment tools to establish a student's readiness for specific occupational courses. CTE teachers can also provide information on the instructional demands (e.g., prerequisite basic, interpersonal, reasoning, and learning-to-learn skills) and setting demands (e.g., independent work, self-monitoring, ability to stay on task). In particular, CTE teachers can provide CTE-specific information. That information would include occupationally specific courses of study, cooperative education, apprenticeship, and career guidance and counselling services.

CTE teachers would also provide any formal programme entry criteria (e.g., prerequisite courses or entry-level skills along with tests to assess them). Although students with disabilities must meet standard programme entry requirements, entry testing must allow any accommodations listed in a student's IEP for test-taking (e.g., extended time, use of a reader).

CTE teachers have a larger responsibility in providing instruction for students with disabilities, particularly school-based experiences. CTE teachers must plan and provide school-based instructional activities that correspond with the goals and objectives of students' IEPs, including classroom and lab activities to teach occupationally specific skills and work-related behaviours. Planning activities that integrate academic and occupational instruction requires collaboration and coordination between CTE and academic teachers.

CTE teachers must also evaluate and grade students' attainment of the IEP objectives on which instruction is based. In addition, CTE teachers must either provide the instructional accommodations and modifications specified in each student's IEP or work with special education personnel who do so. CTE teachers also have an important role to play in providing effective work-based experiences for students with disabilities, which can include field trips, job shadowing, school-based enterprises, career-related camps, apprenticeships, internships, cooperative education, work-study, and part-time job placement.

CTE teachers may share responsibility for contacting local employers; arranging sites and experiences that meet employer and student needs; orienting employers to work-site roles (coaches for instruction, mentors for social initiation and inclusion); visiting sites to observe student work; and monitoring student progress, work, and difficulties. Perhaps most important, CTE teachers must plan and provide the connecting activities that link school- and work-based learning—feedback sessions, discussions, journal writing, student presentations, projects, or portfolios, for example.

To meet the needs of students with disabilities, CTE teachers need background information on students' disabilities and on appropriate accommodations. Accommodations can include modified instructional methods (e.g., repeat and summarise key points, use audiovisual aids, conduct oraltesting or alternative assessments) or equipment (e.g., hand or foot controls, adjustable tables); curriculum objectives might be adapted or supplemented to meet specific student needs.

CTE teachers should identify the assistance available from special educators, tutors, paraprofessionals, or volunteers (e.g., providing print materials in alternative formats, monitoring student work, answering questions, developing teaching aids). So in a nutshell, CTE teachers are one member of the team that helps students with disabilities participate fully and meaningfully in high-quality educational programmes. They play a key role in providing a strong mix of all school programmes – academic, functional, occupational – carefully linked to each other and to work experience, delivered with customised accommodations to meet students' individual needs, and embodying the same high expectations they have of all students.

8

Counselling for Ethnic Minority

Youth from culturally diverse backgrounds often face contrasting notions of self because they must function in schools and educational systems that are organised around the values and goals of the "dominant culture." The dominant culture refers to that of the people who are either the greatest in number or who have the most political and economic power. In the United States, the dominant culture has been defined by white European Americans, specifically those very few who have a great amount of power and wealth.

Students who are not from the dominant culture may be victim to unspoken yet powerful stereotypes and messages about their development and personal identity. Hence, they must learn to negotiate and bridge multiple, and often competing, identities in the schools. Racial and ethnic minority students must learn to operate successfully in the dominant—white—system since they are evaluated based on its norms. This means that children are expected to develop a sense of autonomy and self-reliance and to accept that the individual is seen as the fundamental, or most important, unit of society.

Such understanding of the self as unique has clear implications for how children are treated in school.

Generally speaking, students from collectivistic cultures must learn to be assertive, independent, and confident to succeed in schools, but must also be able to shift back to being relational, modest, passive, and family-oriented in at home. Moreover, home and school contexts are only two of the multiple settings in which students learn to operate across cultures. They must also learn to shift and adapt to culture-based role expectation of peers, elders, significant others, etc..

Those who are unable to adapt to such competing and fluid role demands are often alienated from society. Students from diverse cultural backgrounds learn to adapt to Western cultural norms in the school context in many ways. For example, teachers help them identify internal, personal attributes that make each student different and independent from the another. They emphasise positive attributes in students (intelligence, control, maturity, success) in order to build self-esteem.

Teachers also help orient children to the future by asking them to consider the questions of what will be, or what they could become (future self). This developed sense of individuality, uniqueness, and freedom of choice can be seen in children as early as preschool. Minority group children have more difficulty internalising these aspects of the dominant culture. They show poorer school achievement and have substantially higher dropout rates than majority children, at least in part because of the incongruent expectations, motives, social behaviours, language, and cognitive patterns that teachers and majority students may have.

Student Attitudes Toward Achievement: Non-Western cultures may be characterised by a strong orientation to family and community. Motivation for achievement may come from a desire to gain access to others and to maintain affiliative ties with peers rather than from a desire to attain personal or individual goals. To negotiate competing cultural norms and values, students must learn to be biculturally competent, that is, they must integrate two cultures without feeling the tension between the two. According to the alternation model of bicultural competence, individuals can adapt their behaviour to a given social or cultural context without having to commit to a specific cultural identity.

The ability to adjust across contexts and situations may include using different languages, as well as different problem-solving, coping, interpersonal, communication, and motivational styles of interaction. A way for this orientation to be integrated into the curriculum would be for teachers to introduce more team approaches in the classroom so that children can work together and receive group rewards. Children might be given rewards that enable them to socialise with their peers, or an individualised activity can be paired with a group reward.

Counselling Concerns. Minority cultural values and beliefs, differences in behaviours, language, and worldview, and past power experiences with the dominant culture all influence the success or failure in negotiating identities. For example, how discrepancies in one's sense of self are understood by minority individuals and what is seen as "normal" by the dominant culture may be quite different. The implications of this narrow view of "normality" are that minority individuals are often dismissed or pathologised in comparison to white school children, who are given more long-term support and guidance in schools.

Further, the way that students' "adjustment" – how they bridge competing identities across settings and contexts –

is evaluated in the schools may predetermine an erroneous negative assessment. For example, children may have identity conflicts and question the essence of who they are at school, but function appropriately and effectively at home or vice versa. To help students make a positive social and cultural adjustment, school professionals need an understanding of the students' cultural influences and of the many ways that social and emotional problems which emerge in school are perceived, evaluated, and treated around the world.

Further, counsellors should know the various ways that help is sought out when a problem arises within the family. While children may need help in negotiating their identity or in dealing with other problems, it is not usual for them to seek support services independently; they are referred by teachers and parents, if at all. School personnel must recognise the level of ethnocentrism that influences their evaluation of children, and facilitate positive change in a child that does not involve stereotyping, overgeneralising, or pathologising behaviour that is inconsistent with sanctioned dominant culture.

They also need to realise that because ethnic minority youth must negotiate multiple identities, their youth selves are shifting and fluid, rather than static across home and school settings. Finally, all school personnel must recognise that culture may impact learning style, and consider the social context in which the child is observed, rather than trying to understand behaviours as unequivocal indicators of a child's individual personality or character.

MULTICULTURAL EDUCATION

A comprehensive multicultural education curriculum can

provide students with rich and broad-based knowledge of the subjects covered, foster their understanding and appreciation of ethnic diversity, and promote positive interethnic relations. Multicultural educators need to tailor their curriculum to the developmental level and interests of children and to understand the different needs of majority and minority children. For example, in early childhood young children have concrete thinking and require experiential learning. Therefore, teachers can help them have personal experiences with other groups, share foods, and learn about different customs and holidays.

Adolescents, with abstract thinking skills, can understand diversity through film, literature, and television, and assess how these media contribute to stereotyping, prejudice, and discrimination. Majority children are more likely to be ethnocentric and less aware of ethnic differences. Thus they need more accurate information about other groups and an understanding of the value of diversity in enriching a society. Minority children are typically already familiar with the majority culture, while their own culture has been ignored or disparaged by the curriculum. A better understanding of the strengths and achievements of their own culture will increase their self-esteem.

9

Counselling for Abused Children

Child abuse is the physical or psychological maltreatment of a child by an adult often synonymous with the term child maltreatment or the term child abuse and neglect.

Recognising the Abused Child

Sexual abuse is an uncommonly common thing. It knows no cultural, economic, social or religious barriers. It rears its ugly head in the best of families. Although there is no "typical" victim, those who have suffered this kind of abuse certainly share many behaviours and feelings.

Sexually abused children do not understand their feelings and seldom realise that their ways of behaving are abnormal and/or inappropriate. How the many different kinds of behaviours resulting from incest and sexual abuse manifest themselves often depends on the personalities of individual children and the kinds of experiences that took place. The more traumatised the child is, the more bizarre his or her behaviour will be—and the more extreme the reaction to social interactions.

Because Jeff wanted a more comprehensive list of warning signals, these are:

- extreme reclusiveness, fearfulness, or nonresponsiveness to peer interactions;
- physical and/or emotional difficulties or complaints (nightmares, phobias, stomach pains, venereal infections, etc.);
- violent or highly aggressive behaviours;
- low self-esteem and low self-image;
- vacillation between being pseudo-adult and ultra-immature;
- regressive behaviours (thumb-sucking, clinging, infantile postures, baby talk);
- bedwetting which is not an organic or developmental problem.

Although any one of these symptoms may not, in itself, indicate sexual abuse, all do show that the child is experiencing some kind of physical, emotional or psychological discomfort, and should be checked out. Sexual abuse, whether it occurs "only once or twice" or many times, usually has a critical impact on personality development. Self-esteem suffers immediately, and this is quickly followed by guilt, feelings of helplessness, depression and repressed emotionality.

Academic problems are common among abused children, as are difficulties with concentration and social interactions. Extreme passivity or aggressiveness may be manifested. Their attitudes are often quite punitive and self-destructive. They have experienced a betrayal and a personal violation which should not be, but often is, ignored or discounted in some way. The victimised child adjusts and copes with the situation by assuming responsibility for what has happened. Feelings of shame and self-incrimination have a profound affect on all of his or her future relationships.

Trusting becomes a lifelong problem. It is important for counsellors to provide structure and consistency when dealing with their young clients. Additionally, they give the children explicit permission to be honest in expressing their feelings, and that the counsellors in turn be open and accepting of all that is shared with them. It is important that counsellors, parents and religious leaders alike learn how to identify the various indicators of sexual abuse.

The term "sexual abuse" covers a wide range of behaviours. Some, like an obscene phone call or exhibitionism, are shocking and annoying. Others – incest, rape, child pornography or child prostitution – are more tragic and traumatising. Chronic or ongoing sexual abuse by someone close to the family (a relative, friend or neighbour) can disrupt a child's psychosocial developmental tasks.

Victimised children often develop poor social skills with peers, though they may camouflage this lack by becoming overly gregarious. They are often unable to form anything but very superficial relationships. These children find it extremely difficult to trust people, and are confused as to their sexual roles and identities. Suicide, drugs and alcohol may become avenues of escape for them. Many parents mistakenly believe that their children would never fall for molesters' advances or ploys. But child molesters are highly skilled manipulators and usually mislead adults as well as children.

We have all told our children, "Don't talk to strangers!" But molesters are often not strangers, but relatives, neighbours, family friends or church acquaintances. We need to remember that the sexual abuser is usually known or familiar to the child. A child who is molested by a stranger will probably tell someone about it shortly after it has happened. This child will usually be believed and protected from further abuse. But the victims of ongoing abuse are not so lucky.

Children are taught compliance at an early age. They are instructed to do what an adult or authority figure demands. Most children are awed or intimidated by adults. Perpetrators often convince children that what is going to occur is something very special. Most children do not know that it is wrong or abnormal behaviour. They may feel uncomfortable or sense that what is happening is not OK, but they will usually believe the abuser and discount their own feelings. Once the abuse has begun, the child is hooked into secrecy.

The brighter children are, the more stressful the experience will be for them when they realise that they have been duped. They will feel guilt, shame, helplessness and anger. A statement we often hear from such children is, "I should have known better." Yet how can we expect our children to "know" unless we teach them the skills needed to protect themselves from sexual abuse, just as we teach them other forms of safety? We need to recognise the signs of abuse and to be willing to become advocates for children who are hurting.

We need to listen to our children and to talk to them about sexual abuse. We need to protect them without unduly alarming or scaring them. Parents are not the only ones who find it difficult to talk to children about such abuse. Counsellors, educators, clergy and other clinicians often shy away from asking children—and adults—questions about it. Research indicates that we should be wary of the motives of adults who show an acute interest in our children, and who want to spend a lot of time alone with them. Churches must carefully screen those who work with children. Another precaution is to have co-leaders for youth work. At least one of them should be selected by the congregation, since molesters tend to choose other molesters as their assistants.

In addition, we can educate congregations, Sunday school teachers and other youth personnel about sexual abuse. Children can be taught the difference between "good touch and bad touch," what "private" areas are, and what "lures" child molesters may use. They can learn how to resist getting hooked into something bad that sounds so good! Sexual abuse is not a pleasant topic. It is not a pleasant experience. Guilt, shame, shattered spirits and self-destructive behaviours are its legacy.

Abused children can be found in every city, in every neighbourhood, in every congregation. To deny this or to ignore the warning signs is to help perpetuate the cycle of abuse. Our eyes must be opened and our ears must be trained to hear the silent pleas of the hurting children among us.

Counselling for Abused Children

Counselling abused children is a challenging task for practitioners. The incidence of reported and substantiated child abuse and neglect has risen dramatically since the "discovery" of the Battered Child Syndrome in the sixties, and subsequent mandatory reporting laws. The nation has moved through stages of public awareness about the phenomenon. Currently practitioners have become aware of the widespread sexual abuse of girls (estimated at one in four females) and are developing increasing awareness of the sexual abuse of boys.

Rapid changes in the knowledge base demand that counsellors keep abreast of the indicators of maltreatment, the laws for reporting suspected abuse, and the ways in which children can best be served to overcome effects of a negative family experience. All fifty states require that helping professionals report suspected child abuse to the child protection agency or the police. Many counsellors experience difficulty with reporting requirements for fear of violating the trust of a child, or creating mistrust with the child's parents. Such reporting to Children's Protective Services has saved the lives of many children, and brought help to families.

Although children are still removed from their families and placed in foster homes when it is necessary for their protection, the emphasis has shifted to serving children in their own homes, and providing services to help the family overcome the situations which lead to abuse or neglect. Counsellors should be familiar with child abuse reporting laws in their own states. Typically counsellors and school personnel are required to report suspected abuse, and are granted immunity from liability because they are presumed to be acting in good faith. Many states also have criminal or civil penalties established for mandated professionals who fail to report.

Different Types of Maltreatment

A common theme underlying most forms of maltreatment—physical abuse, neglect, or sexual abuse and exploitation—is that of emotional hurt. The child who is physically abused often suffers emotionally from inconsistent parenting and fear. The sexually abused child suffers from the lack of affection or supervision which leaves him/her vulnerable to the subtle advances of the perpetrator; and the neglected child becomes anxious or apathetic about a life in which basic needs aren't met. One general consequence of child maltreatment is developmental fixation or "freezing." The child who comes to the attention of the counsellor due to difficulties in the classroom or poor social adjustment may very well be a maltreated child.

Neglect

Neglect accounts for more deaths than the physical abuse of children. In a national study of reported child maltreatment, only 4% experienced major physical injury, while 60% experienced a type of physical neglect. Neglect was associated with 56% of child deaths. All types of neglect are essentially a failure by the parents to provide something needed for the child's healthy growth and development. The concept of neglect includes the assumption that some harm must befall the child as a result of the parents' failure to provide.

Physical Abuse

Physical abuse is usually defined as the intentional or nonaccidental inflicting of injury on a child by a caregiver. It manifests as bruises, welts, broken bones, burns, lacerations, or even death. It may occur through hitting, striking, beating, kicking, biting, slapping or other forms of violence directed at a child. Many, if not most, parents who abuse children have been reared in an environment in which some form of maltreatment occurred. Physical abuse appears in all socioeconomic classes, but is correlated with the stresses of poverty.

Sexual Abuse

Child sexual abuse is the adult (or older child) exploitation of the normal childhood development process, through the use of sexual activity. Examples of the types of sexual activity might include touching, kissing, fondling, manipulations of the genitals with the fingers, and actual sexual intercourse. In examining patterns of sexual abuse and exploitation, it is important to keep in mind that the knowledge base is changing rapidly. While earlier belief was that sexual abuse perpetrators were almost always men, McCarty studied female perpetrators and found both accomplices who aided male perpetrators, and independent abusers, who had come from a background of bad childhoods, unhappy marriages and earlier sexual victimisation.

Within the last decade it has been acknowledged that male children are also sexually victimised and are at great risk. It currently appears that female children are more likely to be sexually abused in an incestuous situation, while more male children are sexually abused outside the home.

Emotional Neglect

Emotional neglect generally implies a consistent indifference to the child's needs and covers a range of behaviour, from the parent who never speaks to the child and doesn't remove the child from a crib, to the psychotic parent unable to acknowledge the reality of the child's world, or that the child actually exists. Emotional abuse, on the other hand, implies an active rejection or persecution of the child by the parent. Chronic verbal abuse erodes the child's self-esteem. The use of confinement or excessive punishment is also a form of emotional abuse. Emotional abuse or neglect is usually accompanied by other forms of maltreatment such as sexual abuse or physical abuse. Clearly, children who are being maltreated are not getting their developmental needs met.

Children who have been maltreated are usually unwilling or unable to reveal their situation to a counsellor because of parental threats, or a feeling of loyalty to the family. While sensitive interviewing may help to unearth details of maltreatment, counsellors need to be aware of non-verbal ways in which the message of abuse may be communicated. The presence of one indicator alone does not necessarily mean that maltreatment has occurred. The counsellor looks rather for configurations of indicators. If there are a number of indicators, the counsellor has reason to suspect maltreatment, even if the child has not confided in the counsellor. When abuse is suspected, the counsellor is obligated, under law, to report this concern to Children's Protective Services.

Counselling, in and of itself, cannot ensure the safety of a maltreated child. There will be many professionals involved in working with maltreated children. Typically, a Children's Protective Services worker may coordinate the intervention. Medical personnel will be involved. This may include a coordinating pediatrician who will follow the child's growth and development, several specialists and other health practitioners such as a physical therapist or public health nurse who has worked with the family.

If the child must be removed from the home, the team may include a foster parent. Educators and school personnel are also an important part of the team. They can help to monitor a child's day-to-day safety and progress, and can build programmes to help the child's self-esteem and enhance cognitive development. In dealing with situations where there is risk to a child, the counsellor will find that a team approach accomplishes more for the child than the single intervention of offering counselling.

Child Counselling

One of the primary purposes of counselling the maltreated child is to provide a safe place and safe relationship within which the child may experiment with new adaptations to a safer world, and in which the child's arrested development may become "unstuck." Counsellors cannot literally replace the requisite parental bonding which helps children to grow and develop, but have an opportunity to help the child develop a trusting relationship with an adult. The key to understanding the maltreated child is to look at the developmental stage rather than the chronological age.

The counsellor will be able to identify adaptations which the child made to the maltreatment and teach the child more appropriate ways of interacting. Children often reveal in play the traumatic events of their earlier years. They may also show to the counsellor maladaptive behaviour which puts them at risk of further maltreatment. In the counselling relationship, working with maltreated children requires many techniques other than talking and listening. Using structured or unstructured play situations and artwork, music or clay provide a safe way for children to release tension and express themselves. Younger children do well with dolls and dollhouses to act out family issues for the counsellor.

Many maltreated children have not had normal play opportunities and benefit greatly from free play in the counsellor's office. Using puppets, reading stories, or acting out role plays are ways in which abused children can try out new approaches to relationships. Abused children also do well when counsellors work with them in groups. Younger children do well with developmental play groups, while older children and youth can benefit from activity groups as well as treatment-oriented groups. Group counselling can be especially useful with children and youth who have been sexually abused by reducing their feelings of shame and differentness and helping them to learn how to protect themselves.

Counselling abused children is challenging in that it can arouse many complex feelings within the counsellor. Anger with the child's parents, uneasiness over the child's acting out, or feelings of frustration and sadness are not uncommon for counsellors to face. Anxiety about protecting the children from further maltreatment may be a predominant theme for the counsellor. It is important for counsellors working with the sensitive issues of maltreatment to seek consultation, supervision, or even treatment for themselves when they become overwhelmed with feelings.

Recognising one's professional limitations can also be helpful. It is important to remember that counselling alone cannot protect children, and that any effective long-term intervention will require a concerted team approach and a community which cares enough to offer adequate resources for families. Children will be healed and protected as families are helped.

10

Counselling for Migrant Students

Students who are highly mobile move six or more times in the course of their K-12 education and come from a variety of backgrounds. They include the children of migrant workers, of families experiencing domestic violence, of families in unstable work and home situations that result from high poverty, and of military and immigrant families. High mobility hits urban children particularly hard. Inner city students are more likely to change schools frequently; approximately twenty-five percent of urban third graders were highly mobile compared to approximately one seventh of suburban and rural students.

Some urban schools report student turnover rates from forty to eighty percent. The academic consequences of high mobility are severe. It may take four to six months for mobile students to recover academically from a transfer and they are half as likely to graduate from high school as their non-mobile peers. Many highly mobile students experience isolation after a move, which impacts attendance and performance. Students who move frequently have lower attendance rates: a twenty percent absentee rate has resulted in achievement scores twenty points lower than their stable peers.

Lastly, mobile students are twice as likely to repeat a grade, and mobility even negatively impacts the academic achievement of stable students. Students who live in high poverty and frequently change schools suffer the most academically; however, some categories of highly mobile students (e.g., children of military and immigrant families) are not from low-income families.

Children of migrant workers cross not only school and district lines but multiple state lines, as families follow available work. In 1994 and 2001, Congress addressed the educational needs of this population in legislation that ensures that they are not penalised for lacking continuity in relation to curricula, academic standards and graduation requirements. Subgroups within this population that have additional needs include students with disabilities and older immigrant youth who enter the school system with little prior educational experience.

Despite the fact that most migrant children have parents who work full-time, three-fifths of them live in poverty. These students also have inadequate health care, which contributes to school absences. Migratory children have linguistic and cultural differences, as well as work responsibilities, which tend to isolate. A report published in 2002 found that schools serving a large proportion of limited English proficient migrant students had lower expectations of student performance, less consistent standards and assessments, and less experienced teachers than other schools.

To address this problem, federal programmes such as The Migrant Education Programme (MEP) provide academic and compensatory instruction, support for parental involvement, bilingual and multicultural instruction, vocational instruction, career education services, special guidance counselling and testing services, as well as health and preschool services Migratory students also have delays in education while their families settle in new areas and while their new schools wait for records that indicate the child's appropriate grade placement, educational needs, and health information. As a result, states have instituted programmes, such as the Migrant Student Record Transfer in Texas, to share student information among 46 receiving states that serve migratory children.

Homeless Children

Urban areas have higher concentrations of homeless children than rural and suburban areas; although children in elementary school represent the largest number of homeless children, many secondary school students may not be identified because they no longer attend school, hide their homelessness, or do not access support services. To specifically address the issue of school stability, Congress passed the McKinney-Vento Homeless Education Assistance Act, which allows homeless students to remain in their school of origin (if this is preferred by the family) even if the student no longer lives in the residency area. In addition, schools must provide transportation, if remaining in the school of origin is in the student's best interest.

However, as with migratory students, homeless mobile students often experience delays in their enrolment because of inefficient information transfer and as a result may lose days or weeks of schooling and require many more to catch up. To address this problem, the McKinney-Vento Act requires schools to immediately enroll homeless students and subsequently obtain any missing student information.

Under the McKinney-Vento Act, liaisons build awareness throughout their school districts and community and collaborate with shelter workers and other serviceproviders who work with homeless families and youth to build support networks.

Liaisons must also advocate for unaccompanied youth, including runaways and those not allowed to return to their homes, when the student wishes to enroll in school. In addition to the liaison's efforts, if localities want to access federal funding for housing needs, including shelters and transitional housing, the Department of Housing and Urban Development (HUD) requires the establishment of a Continuum of Care, a network of social service agencies. In communities where the Continuum of Care is well established or in development, local schools should utilise this resource and consider what information is appropriate to place within the system to simplify their outreach to homeless students. School social workers, guidance counsellors, and nurses can also contribute to these services.

Immigrant Family Children

Over half of the foreign born population in the United States is from Latin America, over 25 percent from Asia, and about 16 percent from Europe. Approximately 18 percent speak languages other than English, Spanish being the most common. Many of these families, especially undocumented ones, have members who are rural agricultural workers or urban service and manufacturing workers. Learning to navigate a different system of education and understanding the policies and procedures of American schools add to the number of challenges immigrant youth face as they attempt to get an education.

In addition, communities that attract large numbers of immigrants sometimes act on concerns over lost jobs, "illegal status," and rising social service and educational costs and may seek, as with Proposition 187 in California, to exclude undocumented immigrant children from schools. To counter these initiatives, the Supreme Court ruled in Plyer v. Doe in 1982 that schools may not deny admissions to students on the basis of their residency status.

According to suggestions from the research, schools should also adopt the following procedures to meet the needs of immigrant students: train school personnel in the cultural expectations of the students and families they serve; use bilingual staff to assist non-English speaking parents and students through the admission process; and create admissions policies and procedures that are consistent with immigration laws. In addition, schools should look at strategies and resources that address the significant language barriers that many immigrant students face. Among these are: keeping students with age appropriate peers; avoiding overcorrecting; and assessing academic skills of incoming students in their native language.

Children from Military Families

These highly mobile children have parents who are career military or junior service members in any of the several branches of the U. S. military (Army, Navy, Air Force, Marines, Coast Guard, or National Guard). Thirty-five percent of these students change Department of Defence schools (DoDs) each year; 32 to 50 percent qualify for free or reduced price lunch; and 94 percent of children of enlisted military have parents whose highest education is a high school diploma. Though 90 percent of military families are comprised of two-parent households, the long-term deployment of one parent often forces these military families to function as one-parent households.

Despite the challenges such statistics normally imply, these highly mobile students, unlike migratory or homeless children, consistently perform at academic levels equal to or surpassing the national average for public schools; this high level of achievement includes minority students. Various military branches have devised strategies to address these challenges and to promote academic and social success, which in some case may be useful for other subpopulations. They include: the establishment of family and educational support networks during deployments; the encouragement of parental involvement associated with high academic achievement; the use of school counsellors to meet the needs of military adolescents and to advocate and implement strategies for smoother school transitions; and a "corporate culture" that supports families and encourages strong school-family-military partnerships.

This culture includes high expectations for school success; a welcoming school community; school counsellors trained to understand and advocate for the needs of students; the expectation that parents participate in the child's education through parent meeting attendance and volunteer work.

Migrant Students at the Secondary Level

Measuring exact dropout rates for migrant students is difficult, since their mobility makes accurate counts almost impossible. However, several studies have revealed that most students leave school in the 9th or 10th grade. Surveys of dropouts also show that certain factors are strongly correlated with students' quitting school:

– failure in classes;
– dislike of school;
– extreme lack of credits;
– little involvement in extracurricular activities;
– poor grades;
– extensive migration;
– dislike of school;
– perception of being poorer than other students;
– limited fluency in English;
– history of transiency;
– lack of self-assurance, support and clarity about goals;
– perceived lack of family support and financial pressures;
– overage; lack of interest in school;
– negative parental attitude.

Needs of Secondary Students

The needs of migrant secondary school students are as varied as the students themselves. However, need must be determined in order to design programmes.

Affective Needs are perceived by migrant school staff to be at the root of many students' cognitive failures. Repeated experiences of frustration and failure, and lack of acceptance due to mobility, have produced low self-concept, feelings of isolation, and reduced motivation. Provision of a supportive, positive atmosphere can be highly productive and have great impact on acceptance, goal setting, and role model identification.

Cognitive Needs are specific, practical needs for academic success. They include the following:

- Remedial assistance in math, reading, ESL, etc.
- Study skills development
- Time management
- Academic and vocational guidance

Technical Needs reflect problems which students encounter with school systems and which affect them individually, but over which they have no control:

- Inappropriate age/grade placement. (This is the highest predictor of dropout behaviour, with a 99% dropout rate for students more than one year overage.)
- Credit deficiencies due to frequent moves and no means for earning partial credits.
- Inadequate knowledge of graduation requirements which vary from district to district.

Because addressing the needs of migrant students is a multi-level, multi-faceted undertaking, solutions of many kinds are required. Fortunately, effective solutions are already available.

Direct Services for Assist Migrant Students

Academic Assistance

- *Counselling*: Effective migrant student counsellors pay particular attention to credit completion, graduation requirements, status of competency exams, career and vocational education opportunities, and parental contact.

– *Credit Accrual*: Programmes such as California's Portable Assisted Study Sequence (PASS) enable students to make up or earn extra credits when they are away from school.

– *Tutoring*: Tutoring centres may be used for credit, credit make-up, ESL instruction, and after-hours study. Peer tutors who are also migrant students are especially effective.

– *Extended day/week/year programmes*: Migrant students have proven to be eager to take advantage of after-school, before-school, evening, Saturday, and summer programmes. Migrant Work-Study and Job Training Partnership Act (JTPA) positions can provide after-hours career education and on-the-job training.

– *Special summer programmes*. Many summer programmes provide extracurricular and leadership experiences, and motivate students to seek higher education. Adelante, Yo Puedo, the 4-H Mini-Corps Leadership programme, and the New York State Summer Leadership Conference all provide unique college campus or outdoor experiences for migrant students.

Career Awareness

– work experience programmes have proved to be one of the most powerful prescriptions available to migrant staff trying to cure the dropout syndrome. Such programmes provide the least employable students with an opportunity to learn basic job skills and benefit from the positive effects of the programme. These benefits include ESL practice in a real-life environment, an increased sense of belonging, financial assistance, academic credit, and possible future employment.

- Vocational education can give migrant students valuable opportunities to experience careers other than farmworking.

Alternative Support Programmes

- Cooperative projects are successful in several parts of the country. 4-H, the Cooperative Extension Service's youth programme, assists communities in organising clubs that cover topics ranging from nutrition and crafts to leadership and community service. La Familia is a total educational programme serving the entire migrant family in cooperation with public schools, adult education, and community colleges. Girl and Boy Scouts, YMCA and YWCA, public libraries, health organisations, and private businesses have also worked cooperatively with Migrant Education.
- High school equivalency programmes (HEPs) are designed to serve high school dropouts. Participants earn high school equivalency diplomas through individualised, self-paced study programmes, and receive career and cultural education. Over half of the HEP students are from very low-income migrant families with a prevalence of predictors of educational failure. Yet the programme has met with a great deal of success and enthusiasm from students and educators alike. Between 1980 and 1984, 85% of HEP participants passed their general exams.

Post-secondary Programmes

Even "successful" migrant children are high-risk students, at both high school and college levels. For this reason, several follow-up programmes have been designed to provide continued support.

The College Assistance Migarnt Programme (CAMP) is a Title IV programme that provides tutoring, orientations, and counselling to migrant students planning to enter the university. CAMP success rates are also impressive.

College Bound is a summer programme for high school seniors that helps them make the transition from high school to college. Students study, work, and receive assistance and counselling at a college campus. Over 90% of College Bound students enroll in college the following semester.

Mini-crops is a Migrant education teacher training programme which is designed to provide experience and support for teachers-in-training. Classroom assistance is given to migrant children by a former migrant student who is an identifiable role model.

System level changes involve long-term alterations in the way the educational system serves migrant children. Migrant programmes that work within the system to encourage and train innovative educators can help schools to facilitate, rather than deter, the success of migrant students.

CHANGES AT THE SCHOOL AND DISTRICT LEVELS

— Responsible school policies have included:

a) Credit exchange programmes to accommodate frequent moves;

b) Close monitoring of course credits to prevent deficiencies;

c) Credit completion programmes, partial credit options, and supplementary study programmes to allow for late fall arrivals and early spring departures;

d) In-school alternatives to suspension to avoid unnecessary absences.

– Staff development provides teachers with opportunities to take college courses in relevant areas such as remedial reading, ESL, Spanish language, and cultural differences.

– Role models in schools have a powerful effect on the success of migrant students. Migrant programme workers can encourage the hiring of migrant and bilingual staff.

– Parent involvement is a strong indicator in student success. To involve migrant parents, schools must provide notices to parents in the parents' language; bilingual staff to answer questions; and effective means for communication between parents, students, teachers, administrators.

– Advocacy for student needs is probably the most demanding activity for migrant staff at the high school level. Migrant staff assert the need for appropriate class schedules, test and credit make-up, and special tutoring. They also make student needs known to administrators.

Changes at the Regional and State Levels

– State development. Large districts, regions, counties, and states have the ability to build broad staff development programmes. Statewide programmes are common. They keep migrant staff well-trained in methods of teaching migrant students. Talent exchange policies are effective ways to pass along specialised knowledge.

– Model programmes. State and regional resource centres such as the Educational Resources Information Center (ERIC) help to identify and distribute information on model programmes and special projects in migrant education. These centres may also contain libraries with a variety of migrant-related material.

– Advocacy. The efforts of state and regional programmes can influence changes in migrant education legislation, legal decisions protecting migrant children's rights, and the interstate adoption of programmes such as PASS.

Changes at the Interstate and National Levels

Many organisations and programmes have been created to provide technical assistance for migrant education:

– Migrant Student Record Transfer System (MSRTS) transfers information for migrant students moving between schools.

– Migrant Education Recruitment and Education Taskforce (MERIT) provides advance information to programmes in receiving states about the movement of migrant families.

– Secondary Credit Exchange (SCE) seeks to improve student credit accrual through communication between the home-base and receiving schools.

– National Association of State Directors of Migrant Education (NASDME) investigates current research on migrant education that may prove useful nationwide.

- Migrant Educators' National Training OutReach (MENTOR) provides correspondence courses on educating migrant students.

In addition to these programmes, information dissemination is an important service at the national level. Several projects produce national newsletters.

Programmes for Immigrant Adolescents

Providing appropriate instruction to immigrant students who are English language learners has become an issue of particular concern to educators across the country. This concern is especially acute at the secondary level. A growing number of recent immigrant students are entering U.S. middle and high schools with little or no prior formal schooling and low literacy skills. Often referred to as "late-entrant" or "low-literacy" students, they may be 3 or more years below their age-appropriate grade level in school-related knowledge and skills.

For these students to succeed in school, they must learn to read, write, understand, and speak English; develop academic literacy in English to make the transition to the labour force or into other educational programmes; and become socialised into American society during adolescence, a time of major emotional, physical, and psychological change. The following factors are essential in designing a programme for immigrant adolescents with limited schooling.

Programme Location: A common strategy is to place immigrant English language learners in a specialised learning environment—an all-day or half-day newcomer school or programme, a special wing of a mainstream school, a separate school, separate classes taught in the native language, or classes in which content is taught in English but is adapted and sheltered. Programmes vary in the types of specialised classes offered, the ways in which students are integrated with students from other linguistic and cultural backgrounds and of other ages, and the length of time students attend special programmes or classes before making the transition to mainstream classes.

Some controversy surrounds the question of where to locate these programmes. Separate site programmes have the advantage of consolidating staff and resources, and they can serve a large geographical area while focusing on the special needs of newcomer students. In addition, because all students in the programme are immigrants, no one stands out as a foreigner. Opponents of separate-site programmes believe that they deprive immigrant students of interaction with English-speaking peers and limit access to courses and activities open to students in regular schools.

Opponents also argue that the transition from a separate-site school is harder than the transition from a special programme within a mainstream school. To decide which option is better, local needs and resources must be considered and prior experiences with newcomer students examined.

Programme Structure: The ultimate educational goal for all immigrant students is to perform well in regular content and elective classes. To prepare for academic success, these students need access to courses that focus on literacy and study skills, content courses that are taught through the native language, and sheltered content courses that are taught in English and adapted to make the content more accessible.

Registration and Placement Procedures: Intake centres should be conveniently located, appropriately staffed, and provide essential services. For example, interpreters should be available to interview students and their families in their native languages if necessary. Programmes that serve students from one particular language group should provide registration materials in that language.

Information obtained from registration procedures should be used to make up a student profile, which will serve as an objective basis for determining the student's educational programme. To identify students' needs, it is essential to assess both native language skills and English proficiency and to evaluate prior school experience. In addition, learning about the students' home environments, such as the educational levels of parents and siblings, can help determine the academic support the student has at home.

Transitions to Other Programmes: Some programmes for recent immigrants have come under scrutiny because of their haphasard exit policies. For example, depending on test scores and teacher evaluations, students at newcomer schools in California may be allowed to enter mainstream classes after 8 weeks, 3 semesters, or never. Students who finally are placed in mainstream classes may not receive appropriate support or monitoring. The majority of students move through the newcomer courses in a timely fashion, but few students complete high school in the traditional 8 semesters.

To promote successful transitions, one literacy programme in Fairfax County, Virginia allows students to complete English as a second language (ESL) and sheltered courses at a transitional high school in 1 or 2 years, then proceed to a partial or full mainstream programme to earn their diploma. This progression can be made within 5-6 years of initial registration. Students unable to finish high school by age 22 can fulfil state graduation requirements in adult education courses. Some students in these courses prepare for the General Equivalency Diploma (GED), but most choose to work toward their high school diploma.

Comprehensive Services and Family Involvement. To reach out to parents, schools must find ways to establish regular channels of communication. Effective communication with parents may be hindered by language barriers, parents' lack of familiarity with American schools, and different expectations concerning the appropriate roles of parents and school personnel. To break down such barriers, a programme in Spring Branch, Texas, employs bilingual caseworkers who set up meetings with parents and make home visits. Schools are increasingly coordinating community services and establishing links with the business community and other educational institutions to provide students with a variety of post-secondary opportunities.

Staff Background and Professional Development: Educators who work with immigrant adolescents must maintain academic standards and have high expectations of their students. At the same time, they must teach with sensitivity and compassion and be knowledgeable about their students' language and cultural backgrounds, their personal circumstances and strengths, and their language, literacy, and academic needs. It is important that both ESL and content teachers be familiar with the basic concepts and theories underlying ESL instruction.

Schools should make every effort to hire teachers and classroom aides who share the language and cultural backgrounds of the students or staff with cross-cultural experience and understanding. Mentoring programmes can be set up for teachers and students, and immigrant adults and students who have adjusted to life in the United States can inform teachers about the culture and language of the newcomer students. Traditionally, professional development activities for teachers of immigrant students have been designed for teachers with ESL or bilingual certification. In recent years, however, teachers of mainstream content courses have been included as well. Often, content teachers who have received additional training to work effectively with English language learners teach sheltered content courses.

Although little research has been done on the necessary components of secondary school programmes specifically for students with limited prior schooling, two studies outline features of successful high school programmes for nonnative English speakers in general. Based on a study of six high schools in California and Arizona, Lucas, Henze, and Donato identified characteristics of schools that promote success among students whose first language is Spanish. These characteristics can be extended to apply to programmes serving immigrant students of all backgrounds.

Affective factors. School staff are committed to the educational success of immigrant students, have high expectations for them, and publicly recognise their achievements. Students' native languages and cultures are valued throughout the school, and some of the staff have backgrounds similar to those of the students.

– "Instruction." A wide variety of courses are offered in the students' native languages and in English. This includes advanced content courses made available through instruction in the native language or through sheltered content instruction in English. Teachers are proficient in bilingual and ESL teaching strategies for secondary school students.

– "Comprehensive services." Counsellors speak the students' native languages, have the same or similar cultural backgrounds, and are knowledgeable about post-secondary educational opportunities for immigrant students. In addition, school staff work well with parents and involve them in decisions about their children's education.

– "Professional development." School administrators provide leadership by being knowledgeable about recent research and practice in bilingual and ESL education at the secondary school level and by developing structures to strengthen curriculum and instruction. High priority is placed on professional development for all school staff, and training is designed to help teachers and counsellors serve immigrant students more effectively.

Walsh suggests that a well-designed programme for immigrant adolescents with limited prior schooling and low literacy includes these components:

(1) an ungraded course structure that allows students to learn at their own pace and avoid the stigma of over-age grade placements;

(2) small classes that allow individualised attention from teachers;

(3) literacy and content courses taught in students' native languages that are thematically coordinated and encourage transfer of learning across content areas;

(4) follow-up on thematic content and skill development, provided by double-period ESL classes;

(5) common planning periods that give bilingual and ESL teachers an opportunity to coordinate their work; and

(6) well-defined exit criteria that measure students' readiness for bilingual or mainstream classes.

In addition, Walsh makes the following recommendations:

- Individual learning plans, set jointly by teacher and student, should lead to either a regular or alternative high school diploma. Literacy and content courses should be appropriately designed and taught to enable students to earn full credit toward their diploma. Alternative means of gaining credit (e.g., independent study) and an occupational, career-awareness component that includes hands-on experience should be provided.
- Flexible scheduling should be available, as it enables students to combine academic study and work or work-related experience. Students aged 18 or older can earn a high school diploma by completing at least 2 years in a high school-based programme, then transferring to a GED programme.
- Access to a range of services should be offered, including regular, individual meetings with guidance and adjustment counsellors who speak the students' native languages, group counselling, peer tutoring, mentoring by sympathetic adults, frequent meetings of counsellors with teachers and parents, home-school liaisons, and links with community-based agencies.

11

Multicultural Counselling

There has been growing concern about how best to meet the educational challenge of learner diversity. Some researchers have raised questions about the efficacy of teacher education programmes which attempt to deal with learner diversity and which explore changes in prospective teachers' roles in modifying instruction. However, other researchers have recommended that the following be included within the teacher education curriculum:

- at least one course in multicultural education that takes into consideration the needs of all students;
- information about the history and culture of students from a wide number of ethnic, racial, linguistic, and cultural backgrounds;
- content about the contributions made by various groups;
- information about first- and second-language acquisition and effective teaching practices for working with students from limited English proficient (LEP) backgrounds; and
- field experiences and student teaching opportunities with students from varying backgrounds.

Multicultural Education Courses

Currently there are multicultural education courses across the United States which are used in teacher preparation programmes. The issues raised with respect to educational equality, equity, and social justice within a historical, legal, and sociopolitical context are central to the content. For many prospective teachers, the information provided in these courses is new and has not been discussed in general education courses or in preservice education courses. This background is important for the teacher to have in order to understand the rights and responsibilities of students as well as of teachers and parents.

While having this information may not eliminate the stereotypes or misconceptions that teachers have about groups, it can serve to inform more directly future instructional decisions which they will make. For example, while it may not eliminate some gender beliefs, being aware of the attitudes and perceptions a teacher has about girls and boys and mathematics may diminish sex-segregated groups within the class during math activities.

Information about the History and Culture of Students

Information provided on the history and culture of future students can be a valuable resource for the prospective teacher when making decisions about students, adapting pedagogy, and involving parents. Successful models of open communication between diverse teachers, students, parents, other school personnel, and community liaisons can also be incorporated into teacher education courses. Many African Americans, Hispanics, Native Americans, and Asian Americans have had educational experiences where they suffered as a result of negative social, economic, and educational policies.

Practices such as referral of these students in disproportionate numbers to special education classes continue even today. With additional information, teachers may be able to ask further questions or request technical assistance in providing appropriate instruction before a referral is considered. Some researchers have focused on the miscues which occur between teachers and students based on misinterpretations and generalisations made about cultural background. Student behaviours such as attention-getting strategies, ways of responding to questions, and ways of interacting are examples of actions which are influenced by cultural background.

For some African American, Native American, and Hispanic students, cooperative grouping instructional activities may be better because they parallel the context for learning found in their cultures. Teachers can consider modifying traditional direct instruction to include other types of instruction from which all students can benefit. Another classroom factor to be considered is the extent to which the literacy tradition of the home and culture closely resembles that of the school. If there is a strong emphasis in the culture on the oral tradition, then knowledge may be transmitted through "verbal usage and memorisation" as in the cases of Moroccan and Western Samoan cultures. This is different from the highly literate tradition in the United States and presents problems if the teacher expects certain types of classroom interaction based on reading text.

The cultural values transmitted by parents can be markedly different from those the children encounter in the schools. For example, among some Southeast Asian parents the individual's role within the family is of primary importance; personal desires are secondary. Thus, for these students a decision to care for younger siblings while parents work might come before a decision to complete a school assignment. Understanding child-rearing practices, family relationships, and interpersonal communication is critical in understanding parents.

Communication can be increased by using the home language for conferences and providing written notices in both languages for those parents who have difficulty with English. Community liaisons, aides, translators, or volunteers who are bilingual can assist in this area. The teacher can solicit more participation and cooperation from parents if the message is communicated appropriately.

Integration of Contributions

Modelling the integration of content about the contributions of various groups is vital for prospective teachers because it can demonstrate effective ways of using this information within the classroom. For many students this may be the first opportunity they have had to be exposed to others' national heroes, heroines, events, notable contributions, and theories.

Information about Language

In working with students from varying ethnic and cultural backgrounds, prospective teachers must recognise that many will come from diverse language backgrounds. While there may be a group which can generally be described as "Southeast Asian," these students come from different countries and also speak different languages. The incorporation of information about first- and second-language acquisition and effective teaching practices for working with students from LEP backgrounds is critical for teacher planning.

Information about the language strengths and needs of students will be helpful for working with special personnel such as bilingual teachers and English as a second language teachers. Knowledge about the student's use of both languages can assist the teacher in the development of reading, writing, listening, and speaking skills activities. The teacher may know that one student has contact with English-speaking peers outside of school and also reads material in English at home. Another student may socialise primarily with students from his/her own language background and read materials at home in the native language. This information can be helpful to the teacher in setting up homework assignments as well as in-class interactions with other students.

Importance of Field Experiences

There is a need for field experiences and student teaching opportunities to work with diverse students. Prospective teachers can benefit interacting with these students before they enter the field and while they are still able to dialogue with teacher educators and teachers in the field. It can be a time to design instructional activities which can be applied within a variety of contexts and with different learners. With changes in school populations projected within this decade, it is important for prospective teachers to also have contact with the populations which they will ultimately serve.

Counselling for Communication Disorders in Culturally Diverse Students

Accurate assessment of culturally and linguistically diverse students is difficult in any area. Assessing the speech and language skills of these students is even more challenging. For any student, communication skills are disordered if they deviate sufficiently from the norms and expectations of the student's speech community.

The challenge with culturally and linguistically diverse students is that many of the traditional assessment tools and benchmarks are not based upon their speech communities. Instead, they generally are based upon the "mainstream" or "standard" dialect of American English, known as "Standard American English" (SAE). While it is critical that students acquire this dialect, evaluators cannot identify students with a communication disorder because they speak a different dialect.

The limitations of speech and language tests in accurately discriminating typical and impaired language speakers of SAE are widely known. So, before reporting any test scores, the evaluator analyses the test's quality and applicability. To do this, the evaluator considers:

- Construct validity. How accurate is the test in distinguishing typically developing students from students with communication disorders?
- Content validity. Do the test items make sense?
- Normative sample. Did significant numbers of the subjects used to norm the test have similar linguistic and cultural backgrounds as the student being evaluated?

– Reliability. Are the test results consistent for a student even if the test is given again or given by a different evaluator?

An analysis of the quality and applicability of currently available tests reveals that none meets acceptable standards. The use of scores derived from such tests causes inaccurate identification of students with communication disorders, which has "serious" "social consequences".

With English language learners, the use of translated versions of speech and language tests pose even greater problems. For example, many translations provide word-for-word translations which do not account for a lack of equivalent linguistic forms in the second language. Additionally, translated tests do not consider the effects of second language acquisition on a student's performance. As a result, scores from these translated versions should not be used to diagnose a communication disorder.

Determine of Communication Disorder

Before deciding whether a communication disorder exists, the evaluator first accumulates a good deal of information about the student's communication skills. The evaluator approaches this phase as both an anthropologist and a detective. Critical information includes:

– Comprehensive data concerning the student's significant current and past exposure to particular languages and dialects, and consideration of the student's proficiencies in those languages and dialects.
– Data about the student's speech and language skills in a number of settings and covering different types of language, such as social language and more demanding uses such as for comparison, synthesis, and

problem solving. This can be gathered by direct observation and elicitation, by interviewing people who can provide that information, and by reviewing historical information on the student's speech and language skills.

- Parent/long-time caregiver reports (this may be the most valuable information) including:
  a) Developmental history and significant medical history;
  b) Information on the parent's education and;
  c) The parent's judgment as to:
     1. how the student's speech and language development compares to his/her siblings at the same age, or to the student's peers in his/her speech community;
     2. whether there is a history of speech-language problems in the student's family and/or;
     3. whether there is a history of academic problems in the student's family.
- Teacher interviews and portfolio reviews on overall school performance, both currently and historically.
- Tasks designed to probe particular areas of speech and language, whether using standardised or nonstandardised tools, including:
  a) Grammatical development compared to the norms of the student's speech community;
  b) Ability to comprehend and integrate information the student hears and reads in his/her school and community;

c) Ability to organise and integrate ideas and information so the student can express himself/herself when participating in classroom discussions and in written work;

d) Development of curriculum-based language skills such as phonological awareness, language-based memory skills, vocabulary development, and language-based literacy and math skills.

— Information on the student's ability to learn, generally elicited through dynamic assessment methods, to aid in determining whether the student's incorrect response was due to a lack of prior exposure to the test's task requirement or content, or a true communication disorder.

After all the critical information is gathered, the evaluator analyses a number of factors to determine whether any apparent difficulties are due to a true communication disorder or to something else-such as a communication difference or a lack of prior exposure. To make this differential diagnosis, the evaluator applies available research on the norms of a student's speech community. Often the research is limited. The evaluator applies his/her own knowledge base, and may enlist the help of someone who knows the student's linguistic and cultural background and who can, with proper training, provide valuable information on these critical factors:

— Sociolinguistics. The evaluator considers how social and cultural factors might have influenced the quality and quantity of information gathered. For example, a student might be reticent to talk

1) with an adult she/he does not know,

2) about something the student is not interested in, or

3) in an unfamiliar setting.

The evaluator also considers how the particular information-gathering tasks might be culturally unfamiliar to the student. Depending on the student's speech community, examples of unfamiliar tasks might include tasks requiring that the student

1) answer questions that the evaluator already knows the answers for;
2) tell stories if the student did not have experience telling or hearing stories; or
3) label objects when that is not commonly done at home.

– Prior educational experiences. The evaluator distinguishes between the effect of poor educational experiences and a true communication disorder. Substandard school instruction may impact many aspects including the fund of general knowledge, vocabulary skills, problem solving skills, literacy skills, and, of course, success in meeting curriculum standards.

– Linguistics. The evaluator adjusts his/her linguistic criteria based upon characteristics of second language learning; amount and quality of exposure to various dialects the student produces; and variations as to when certain developmental benchmarks are met in different languages and dialects. This linguistic knowledge also enables the evaluator to distinguish an accent from an articulation or phonological delay.

In the end, the evaluator analyses the data to determine

– whether the student has a communication disorder, and

– if so, the level of severity of that disorder.

The written report contains sufficient information, including quoting and describing actual speech and language performance data, to enable a reader to understand how the evaluator forms his/her clinical judgment, based upon an analysis of all the accumulated information.

Counselling for Multiracial Students

Anxiety is a basic human emotion consisting of fear and uncertainty that typically appears when an individual perceives an event as being a threat to the ego or self-esteem. While everyone may have occasional moments of feeling anxious or worried, an anxiety disorder is a medical condition that causes people to feel persistently, uncontrollably worried over an extended period of time. The disorder may result in significant distress in a number of settings, such as school, peer relationships, and home life, and it may dramatically affect people's lives by limiting their ability to engage in a variety of activities. Anxiety that occurs in multiple settings, involving excessive apprehension about a number of situations on most days is known as a generalised anxiety disorder.

Generalised anxiety disorder (sometimes known as GAD) affects approximately three to four percent of children. Other anxiety disorders, which are triggered by more specific situations, include:

– social phobia or social anxiety: fear of meeting new people or of embarrassing oneself in social situations
– specific phobia: fear of a particular object (for example, spider) or situation (for example, airplane travel)

- separation anxiety disorder: fear of separating from home or primary caregiver
- panic disorder: unpredictable and repeated panic attacks unrelated to surrounding circumstances
- obsessive-compulsive disorder: uncontrollable, repetitive, thoughts and fears, often accompanied by repetitive behaviours intended to prevent the fears from being realised
- selective mutism: persistent failure to speak in specific social situations (despite the physical ability to speak in other situations), most likely due to severe social anxiety

The tendency to develop any anxiety disorder involves complex genetic and environmental factors, and it is possible for one person to have more than one anxiety disorder.

Generalised Anxiety Disorder

Children with generalised anxiety disorder are often preoccupied with worries about their success in activities and their ability to obtain the approval of others. These children may have persistent thoughts of self-doubt that they are unable to control, and they constantly criticise themselves. Children may be preoccupied with being on time to events and insist on doing a task "perfectly." In contrast to the ordinary, occasional worries or fears experienced in childhood, generalised anxiety disorder persists for at least six months and affects children throughout the day (at home, at school, and with friends).

Children may appear inflexible or excessively worried about conforming to rules, or they may not be able to enjoy hobbies or other recreational activities. Some children may appear shy when, in fact, they are preoccupied with significant worries. Even if children are aware that their worries are more intense than is warranted by a situation, they may not be able to stop the worry. A trained clinician (such as a child psychiatrist, child psychologist or pediatric neurologist) should integrate information from home, school, and the clinical visit to make a diagnosis. At home, children with generalised anxiety disorder may have a combination of the symptoms listed below.

- Excessive worry and anxiety about a variety of matters on most days for at least 6 months. Children may worry about school tasks, interactions with peers, being on time, and following rules. Worry about receiving approval is common. Children may worry about future activities, new experiences, or many other matters.
- Frequent self-doubt and self-critical comments
- Inability to stop the worry despite parental reassurance
- Physical problems, including headaches, stomach ache, fatigue, and muscle tensions
- Signs of persistent anxiety, including restlessness, feeling "on edge," difficulty concentrating or relaxing, or mind going blank
- Irritability, which often increases with increased worry
- Sleep problems, which may include waking up early, waking up feeling unrested, or trouble falling asleep or staying asleep
- Experimentation with alcohol or drugs as a way to reduce suffering. Drugs and alcohol can themselves produce or worsen anxiety.

- Depression or thoughts of not wanting to be alive in some situations if children believe there is no hope of reducing their symptoms

At school, a child with generalised anxiety disorder may have a combination of the symptoms listed below.

- Excessive worry and anxiety about a variety of matters
- Repeated seeking of teacher approval
- An inability to explain the worries. Children may not understand why they are so anxious.
- Inability to stop the worry. Despite adult reassurance, the worries continue.
- Difficulty transitioning from home to school. Children may develop difficulty entering school in the morning if they associate more worries with school. This may lead to late arrival times, long and tearful morning drop-offs, or tearful episodes at school.
- Refusal or reluctance to attend school. Anxiety may lead a child to insist on staying at home.
- Avoidance of academic and peer activities
- Self-criticism and low self-esteem
- Difficulty concentrating due to persistent worry, which may affect a variety of school activities, from following directions and completing assignments to paying attention
- Other conditions, such as attention deficit hyperactivity disorder (ADHD), may also be present, compounding learning difficulties. Having one mental health condition does not "inoculate" the child from having other conditions as well.

– Other anxiety disorders, such as social phobia, separation anxiety, or panic disorder. Anxiety disorders may not be recognised both because children may try to hide symptoms and because their symptoms are experienced internally and may not be easily seen.

– Learning disorders may co-exist and should not be overlooked in this population. A child's difficulties in school should not be presumed to be due entirely to anxiety. If the child still has academic difficulty after symptoms are treated, an educational evaluation for a learning disorder should be considered. A child's repeated reluctance to attend school may be an indicator of an undiagnosed learning disability.

– Side effects from medications. Medications may have cognitive or behavioural effects or physically uncomfortable side effects that interfere with school performance. After a child begins receiving medical treatment for symptoms, any mood changes or new behaviours should be discussed with parents, as they can reflect medication side effects.

A child's symptoms of generalised anxiety may be evident during an office visit when a child is reluctant to meet the clinician. This feature alone does not indicate a child has anxiety, since children routinely are nervous during office visits. Clinicians may benefit from talking with parents, school staff, and other important caregivers to evaluate a child's functioning in each area to determine the underlying cause of the child's symptoms. Clinicians may encounter some of the following challenges in diagnosing and treating a child or adolescent with generalised anxiety.

– Symptoms vary over time and their appearance changes as a child grows. A clinician may need to see a child over time to determine the appropriate diagnosis.

- Other anxiety disorders may look like generalised anxiety disorder
- Symptoms of mood disorders, such as depression and bipolar disorder, and behaviour disorders, such as attention deficit hyperactivity disorder, can resemble the symptoms of anxiety. Depression is often identified in these children.
- Certain medical conditions can cause anxiety. These conditions include hyperthyroidism, hyper-parathyroidism, hypoglycemia, cardiac disorders, seizure disorders, gastrointestinal problems, and vestibular or inner-ear disorders. Relevant laboratory tests and physical examinations may be helpful when a child has anxiety.
- Caffeine and other substances, such as stimulants, can produce anxiety. Consequently, evaluation for caffeine use and other substance use, especially with adolescents, is important.
- Physical complaints such as stomach aches, headaches, and dizziness often occur in children with anxiety. The clinician must determine whether these complaints warrant further medical investigation.
- Children may have difficulty talking about their worries. Phrasing questions with particular sensitivity and compassion may allow a more complete picture of symptoms to emerge.
- Children may be unaware, or unwilling to admit, that their feelings or behaviour may indicate symptoms of a disorder

– Families may need to be coached about what they can reasonably expect from their child. Children who suffer from any anxiety disorder will benefit if their family understands that therapy and medicines may reduce, but may not cure, symptoms.

Treatment for Generalised Anxiety

Generalised anxiety disorder is treatable through ongoing interventions provided by a child's medical practitioners, therapists, school staff, and family. These treatments include psychological interventions (counseling), biological interventions (medicines), and interventions at home and at school to reduce sources of stress for the child. Open, collaborative communication between a child's family, school, and treatment professionals optimises the care and quality of life for the child with anxiety.

Counselling

Counselling can help children with anxiety, and everyone around them, to understand that their symptoms are caused by a disorder with complex genetic and environmental origins—not by flawed attitude or personality. Counseling also can reduce the impact of symptoms on daily life. Relaxation training can teach the child how to reduce both the worries and the accompanying physical symptoms. A variety of psychological interventions can be helpful, and parents should discuss their child's particular needs with their clinician to determine which psychological treatments could be most beneficial for their child.

– Individual psychotherapy is generally recommended as the first line of treatment for children and adolescents with generalised anxiety disorder. Children with anxiety may carry a sense of failure, as if the disorder was their fault. Individual psychotherapy can help reduce symptoms, and can help young people to become aware of and address their feelings of failure and self-blame.

– Cognitive Behaviour Therapy (CBT) can teach young people new skills to reduce anxiety. In CBT, a child or adolescent is helped to become aware of and to describe anxiety-laden thought patterns. A trained clinician guides the child to think of new, more positive patterns of thinking. The young person is then given a chance to practice using these new thought patterns outside the clinical visit, and to discuss his or her experiences with the clinician afterwards. These methods are based upon well-researched practices that have helped many children and adolescents.

– Parent guidance sessions can help parents to manage their child's illness, identify effective parenting skills, learn how to function as a family despite the illness, and to address complex feelings that can arise when raising a child with a psychiatric disorder. Family therapy may be beneficial when issues are affecting the family as a whole.

– Group psychotherapy can be valuable to a child by providing a safe place to talk with other children who face adversity or allowing a child to practice social skills or symptom-combating skills in a carefully structured setting.

– School-based counseling can be effective in helping a child with anxiety navigate the social, behavioural, and academic demands of the school setting.

Biological interventions

While psychotherapy may be sufficient to treat some

children with anxiety, other children's symptoms do not improve significantly with psychotherapy alone. These children may benefit from medications. The U.S. Food and Drug Administration (FDA) has not approved specific medications for the treatment of generalised anxiety disorder in children and adolescents. However, medications approved by the FDA for other uses and age groups are prescribed for young people with generalised anxiety disorder. The FDA allows doctors to use their best judgment to prescribe medication for conditions for which the medication has not specifically been approved.

The antidepressants Celexa, Lexapro, Luvox, Paxil, Prozac (fluoxetine), and Zoloft are commonly prescribed to treat the symptoms of anxiety. These medicines belong to a group of medications called Selective Serotonin Reuptake Inhibitors, or SSRI's. In most cases these medicines begin to be effective in reducing symptoms after the child or adolescent has taken them for at least 2-4 weeks. Fully 12 weeks may be required in order to determine whether the medication is going to be effective for a particular individual. Medications should only be started, stopped, or adjusted under the direct supervision of a trained clinician.

There is no "best" medicine to treat generalised anxiety disorder, and it is important to remember that medicines usually reduce rather than eliminate symptoms. Different medicines or dosages may be needed at different times in a child's life or to address the emergence of particular symptoms. Successful treatment requires taking medicine daily as prescribed, allowing time for the medicine to work, and monitoring for both effectiveness and side effects. The family, clinician and school should maintain frequent communication to ensure that medications are working as intended and to monitor and manage side effects. The following cautions should be observed when any child or adolescent is treated with antidepressants.

- Benefits and risks should be evaluated. Questions have arisen about whether antidepressants can cause some children or adolescents to have suicidal thoughts. The evidence to date shows that antidepressants, when carefully monitored, have safely helped many children and adolescents. Consideration of any medicine deserves a discussion with the prescribing clinician about its risks and benefits.
- Careful monitoring is recommended for any child receiving medication. Though most side effects occur soon after starting a medicine, adverse reactions can occur months after medicines are introduced. Agitation, restlessness, increased irritability, or comments about self-harm should be addressed immediately with the clinician if any of these symptoms emerge after the child starts an antidepressant. Frequent follow-up (weekly for the first month) is now advocated by the FDA for children starting an antidepressant.
- Some children who have generalised anxiety disorder may also have bipolar disorder. In some individuals with bipolar disorder, antidepressants may initially improve depressive symptoms but can sometimes worsen manic symptoms. While antidepressants do not "cause" bipolar disorder, they can unmask or worsen manic symptoms.

Interventions at home

At home, as well as at school, providing a sympathetic and tolerant environment and making some adaptations may be helpful to aid a child or adolescent with anxiety.

– Understand the illness. Understanding the nature of anxiety and how it is experienced by the child will help parents sympathise with a child's struggles.

– Listen to the child's feelings. Isolation can foster low self-esteem and depression in children struggling with anxiety. The simple experience of being listened to empathically, without receiving advice, may have a powerful and helpful effect.

– Keep calm when a child becomes anxious about an event or matter. If a child sees a parent is able to remain calm, the child can model the parent's attitude.

– Reassure the child and gently note that he or she survived prior situations that caused anxiety.

– Teach relaxation techniques, including deep breathing, counting to 10, or visualising a soothing place. Teaching children how to relax can empower them to develop mastery over symptoms and improve a sense of control over their body.

– Plan for transitions. Getting to school in the morning or preparing for bed in the evening may be complicated by fears and anxieties. Anticipating and planning for these transition times may be helpful for family members.

– Support the child's quick return to school, in the case of school refusal. The best way to reduce anxiety about school is to address specific causes of anxiety and help the child return to school as quickly as possible. A shorter school day may help until symptoms improve. Children's symptoms are more likely to decrease when they discover that they can survive the anxiety. Long absences are likely to cause higher levels of anxiety upon returning.

- Encourage the child's participation in activities that may provide a reprieve from worries
- Praise the child's efforts to address symptoms. Young people often feel that they only hear about their mistakes. Even if improvements are small, every good effort deserves to be praised.
- Encourage the child to help develop interventions. Enlisting the child in the task will lead to more successful strategies and will foster the child's ability to problem-solve.

Interventions at school

There are many ways that schools can help a child with generalised anxiety disorder succeed in the classroom. Meetings between parents and school staff, such as teachers, guidance counsellors, or nurses, will allow for collaboration to develop helpful school structure for the child. The child may need particular changes (accommodations/ modifications) within a classroom. Examples of some accommodations, modifications, and school strategies include the following:

- Establish check-ins on arrival to facilitate transition into school
- Accommodate late arrival due to difficulty with transitions
- Because transitions may be particularly difficult for these children, allow extra time for moving to another activity or location. When a child with anxiety refuses to follow directions, for example, the reason may be symptoms of anxiety rather than intentional oppositionality.

– If the child is avoiding school, determine the cause of the child's reluctance and address it, initiate a plan to for him or her to return to school as quickly as possible. It may help ease anxiety if the child attends for a shorter school day temporarily.

– Identify a "safe" place where the child may go to reduce anxiety during stressful periods. Developing guidelines for appropriate use of the safe place will help both the student and staff.

– Develop relaxation techniques to help reduce anxiety at school. Employing the techniques developed at home can be useful.

– Provide alternative activities to distract the child from physical symptoms. Calming activities may be helpful.

– Encourage small group interactions to develop increased areas of competency

– Provide assistance with peer interactions. An adult's help may be very beneficial for both the child and his or her peers.

– Encourage the child to help develop interventions. Enlisting the child in the task will lead to more successful strategies and will foster the child's ability to problem-solve.

– Reward a child's efforts. Every good effort deserves to be praised.

Flexibility and a supportive environment are essential for a student with generalised anxiety disorder to achieve success in school. School faculty and parents together may be able to identify patterns of difficulty and develop remedies to reduce a child's challenges at these times.

Test Anxiety

One of the most threatening events that causes anxiety in students today is testing. When students develop an extreme fear of performing poorly on an examination, they experience test anxiety. Test anxiety is a major factor contributing to a variety of negative outcomes including psychological distress, academic underachievement, academic failure, and insecurity. Many students have the cognitive ability to do well on exams but may not do so because of high levels of test anxiety. Because of the societal emphasis placed on testing, this could potentially limit their educational and vocational opportunities.

Test anxiety is composed of three major components: cognitive, affective, and behavioural. Students who experience test anxiety from the cognitive perspective are worriers lacking self confidence. They may be preoccupied with negative thoughts, doubting their academic ability and intellectual competence. Furthermore, they are more likely to overemphasise the potential negative results and feel helpless when in testing situations.

Some students may feel the need to answer every question on the test correctly. When this does not occur they may think of themselves as being incompetent, thus fueling negative thoughts such as, "I knew I was not going to pass this test," "I know I am going to make a poor grade," or "Everyone knows I am not smart." In order for students to have the best opportunity for academic success, negative thinking must be minimised and controlled.

From the affective perspective, test anxiety causes some students to experience physiological reactions such as increased heart rate, feeling nauseated, frequent urination, increased perspiration, cold hands, dry mouth, and muscle spasms. These reactions may be present before, during, and even after the test is completed. In conjunction with the physiological reactions, emotions such as worry, fear of failure, and panic may be present. When students are not able to control their emotions, they may experience higher levels of stress, thereby making it more difficult for them to concentrate.

Test-anxious students express anxiety behaviourally by procrastinating and having inefficient study and test-taking skills. Zeidner contends that test-anxious students have a more difficult time interpreting information and organising it into larger patterns of meaning. In addition, some students may physically feel tired or exhausted during test administration because they do not have a healthy diet, have poor sleeping habits, and fail to routinely exercise.

Suggestions for Overcome Test Anxiety

There are a number of suggestions that school administrators, teachers, school counsellors, and parents may utilise to help students effectively manage test anxiety.

Administrators should:

- attempt to build a strong alliance with parents, students and teachers by explaining to them the importance of testing including potential advantages and disadvantages.
- encourage teachers to teach the curriculum rather than teaching to the test because ideally the test should reflect the curriculum being taught.
- develop school policies on standardised tests that are clear and easily understood.
- consider giving students school-wide practice tests.

- encourage school counsellors to address test anxiety with students individually, in small groups, and during classroom guidance lessons.

Teachers should:

- become aware of students' developmental levels and the pressure they may be placing on students prior to test administration.
- teach students successful test-taking strategies that include understanding test time limits, the importance of pacing, and the different type of test formats (e.g. multiple choice, essay, fill in the blank).
- consider designing some classroom tests using the standardised test format during the school year.
- help students understand test ceilings and provide information on whether or not they will be penalised for incorrect responses. If points are deducted for incorrect responses students should be informed to leave items blank.
- address test anxiety in class by exploring students' concerns and, if necessary, meet with the school counsellor and parents of identified students to confront this issue.

School counsellors should:

- collaborate with school officials to identify students experiencing test anxiety.
- conduct classroom guidance topics on test anxiety, test-taking strategies, and effective study skills, and consult with teachers.
- practice different forms of relaxation techniques with students and provide them with the cognitive tools to

defeat the negative self-talk they may experience before, during, and after the test.

- offer workshops to parents focusing on ways they may help their children reduce test anxiety.
- meet with students experiencing test anxiety individually or in small groups to address this issue in more detail.
- seek out students who have successfully defeated test anxiety and have them speak or partner with other students to share their experience.
- be aware of the developmental levels of students and recognise when test anxiety is out of control, because more serious anxiety-related problems could be present

Parents should:

- make sure their children attend school regularly.
- create and maintain a home environment that will help their children be well rested during regular school days and during the week of testing.
- evaluate their children's academic progress over a period of time rather than on one single test score.
- talk with their children and encourage them to do their best.
- be proactive, contact school officials if they have questions concerning tests results.
- encourage their children to maintain a healthy diet and exercise on a regular basis.

Students are encouraged to:

- consistently develop good sleeping habits, especially during the week of the test, and maintain a healthy diet and exercise regularly.

– avoid cramming, develop good study habits and good test taking skills.
– wear comfortable clothes during the exam and maintain a comfortable and relaxed body posture during the test.
– be aware of time allotted for the test, read directions carefully, and for time management purposes leave questions blank that they are not sure of and attempt to answer them later.
– not compare themselves to other students while taking the test.
– take deep breaths and attempt to regain composure when anxiety levels are high or when negative thoughts are present.

Multiracial individuals have been stereotyped as socially inept individuals who lack culture and are destined to have social and psychological problems associated with racial identity, thus leading a confused life because they will never fit in or gain acceptance to any racial group. According to Brown, to automatically suggest that multiracial individuals will likely have identity problems as a result of their background typically refers to the view that these individuals do not fit neatly into socially defined racial categories and as a result they have trouble determining their position, role, and status in society.

It is important for school counsellors to treat multiracial students as individuals first and avoid making false assumptions about them based upon characteristics associated with multiracial group membership. Another stereotype associated with multiracial individuals is the belief that they are more accepted in the minority community and should therefore identify with the parent of colour. This perspective is associated with elements of the "one drop rule," which originated from the belief that each race had its own specific blood type and just one drop of "Negro blood" provided enough evidence to classify that person as black, regardless of their physical appearance.

The ultimate goal behind the "one drop rule" was to promote segregation and discourage social interaction between blacks and whites. However, when multiracial individuals do not culturally identify with both parents, Sebring contends this may cause them to experience feelings of disloyalty and enormous guilt over their rejection of one parent for the other. Therefore it is crucial for multiracial children to assume a multiracial identity. Finally, some believe that multiracial individuals do not like to discuss their racial heritage. On the contrary, Kerwin and Ponterotto indicated that when multiracial individuals are approached in a genuine and caring manner, they do not mind such inquiries and may associate this interest with acceptance and support.

School counsellors should first develop an awareness of their own personal feelings toward multiracial individuals and multiracial families. If erroneous or preconceived notions exist about multiracial children or multiracial families, they must be confronted and emotionally resolved if school counsellors are to maximise their effectiveness. School counsellors should also strive to educate themselves about the emotional needs of multiracial children by reading literature, attending workshops, and talking with multiracial families.

The American Academy of Child and Adolescent Psychiatry (AACAP) reports that research focusing multiracial individuals has shown that:

1) multiracial children have similar self-esteem levels and experience psychiatric problems at no greater rate when compared to other children;

2) the racial identity of children from the same multiracial family can vary because identity is influenced by factors including family attachments, family support, experiences with diverse racial and ethnic groups, and individual physical features;

3) multiracial children may develop a public identity with the minority race yet also hold a private multiracial identity with family and friends as a way to cope with societal prejudice;

4) multiracial children may encounter obstacles that make it more difficult for them to accept and value the culture of both parents when parents divorce; and

5) multiracial individuals who possess a true multiracial identity are raised in an environment incorporating the values and beliefs of both racial groups and are generally happier than multiracial individuals who identify with the race of only one parent.

Multiracial individuals, because of their unique developmental history, will typically possess more insight and sensitivity to both racial groups than single race children because they have the opportunity to personally experience what the racial identity of each implies.

School counsellors should become knowledgeable about the different developmental aspects of racial identity for multiracial individuals. Models developed by Poston and Kerwin and Ponterotto are helpful resources to school counsellors as they learn about this population of students. Learning how to promote the racial identity development of multiracial children is also a common issue for parents.

Parents tend to:

(1) deny or minimise the significance of race as an important factor in identity development,

(2) incorporate the identity of only one parent by immersing the family solely in that parent's particular community, or

(3) encourage multiracial children to embrace all aspects of their multiracial heritage.

McRoy and Zurcher identified a number of significant factors that help facilitate the positive development of racial identity of multiracial children:

- Multiracial children should be encouraged to acknowledge and discuss their racial heritage with their parents, extended family members, and other important individuals in their lives.
- Parents must be able to perceive their child's racial heritage as being different from their own. They should be willing to make changes that will contribute to the development of a positive racial identity in the child.
- Multiracial children should be given the opportunity to develop relationships with people from culturally diverse backgrounds. This can be accomplished by attending a culturally diverse school and by living in a culturally diverse neighbourhood.
- The family should form an identity as a multiracial unit.

These factors are significant because even though societal attitudes towards multiracial families and multiracial individuals have improved, stereotypes and prejudice are still likely to be confronted. Harris found that school counsellors validated this perspective. They strongly believed that schools are a microcosm of a society that does not genuinely accept multiracial children, thus the question follows: how genuinely are multiracial children accepted in schools? The multiracial population in the school setting will continue to increase as our nation's population becomes more diverse. Therefore it is important for school counsellors to have an accurate understanding of multiracial individuals and their families.

School counsellors should work to create a cultural environment in their school setting that embraces diversity because, as Harris found:

- School counsellors who were employed in schools that actively promoted cultural diversity and awareness programmes held more accurate perceptions of multiracial children.
- School counsellors who were in schools that did not actively promote cultural diversity and awareness programmes were more likely to inaccurately:
    1) believe that racial identity issues were the major cause of emotional problems for multiracial children,
    2) support the perception that multiracial children should identify primarily with the minority parent, and
    3) categorise multiracial children with the minority parent.
- School counsellors in school settings that actively promoted cultural diversity and awareness programmes believed living in a racially diverse neighbourhood was helpful in facilitating positive development of racial identity for multiracial children.

12

Counselling for Violent Situation

The celebration of violence in movies, on television, and in popular songs has turned into an epidemic of personal tragedies for people living in our Nation's cities. Exacerbated by the ready availability of drugs and weapons, violence has become a public health issue of immediate concern. Yet the sources of violence are deep and longstanding, for ours is a country sharply divided between haves and have-nots; and areas of high poverty concentration have long been susceptible to all forms of violence, from vandalism, robbery, and rape, to suicide—the ultimate violence of despair.

People who grow up in poor urban neighbourhoods tend to be surrounded by unemployed adults, rundown housing, a physically deteriorated environment, and the constant fear of crime. Too often their own parents are ill-prepared, neglectful, or even abusive—children, like them. And the paucity of good role models in the community and at school contributes to young people's belief that the deck is stacked against them. Not surprisingly, these youth experience a free-floating anger, accompanied by feelings of frustration and helplessness, making them tinder boxes, ready to ignite at any provocation.

Surrounded by violence in their homes and neighbourhoods, as well as in the society at large, youth often look to the school as a haven. Indeed, the most resilient are students who can use their teachers and other staff as mentors and role models, and their time at school as a profitable refuge. Unfortunately, large urban schools are themselves often anonymous, alienating, and fraught with danger. Insofar as the schools mirror the society, they can exacerbate the problem of violence in several key ways:

Influence of Impoverished Neighbourhoods and Schools

Because schools are largely funded by property taxes, the school districts that face the toughest challenges from the students they serve are also those with the fewest funds to meet their children's needs. Schools in poor, deteriorated, crime-ridden neighbourhoods tend to be physically dilapidated, overcrowded, and lacking the resources necessary for effective teaching. Not only are classes much larger than in affluent neighbourhoods, but students sit at broken desks, and teachers (who are often less well paid than their suburban colleagues) must do without laboratory equipment, computers, and even the most elementary supplies like chalk and books.

Urban students are aware that their schools are rundown and poorly equipped in comparison with suburban schools, that the technology isn't up-to-date enough to prepare them for jobs or college, and that they are often distrusted and feared by the adults who work with them. When these same students are able to go to school in well-equipped, modern buildings, they score higher academically than their peers in the old rundown schools. In fact, in several cities, when old schools were renovated or new schools built, students' test scores showed marked academic improvement.

Influence of Large Schools and Classes

The inability of teachers and other school staff to make meaningful connections with students in large schools and increasingly large classes has become a key safety issue. Adolescence is universally a precarious developmental stage, and many teenagers have limited reserves of self-esteem. Given the enormous problems urban students face, they see little hope for their future. Although urban adolescents want contact with adults, too often they are deprived of sustained relationships with caring adults in their homes and neighbourhoods.

Unfortunately, even elementary school teachers must struggle against large classes to pay adequate attention to their students, and teachers in junior highs and secondary schools often see 150-200 students a day. Thus teachers inadvertently become yet another lost opportunity for connection. Without sustained contact, they cannot give their students a vision of what education can offer, or save them from self-destructive behaviour. Indeed, many educators are convinced that, without reducing class size, all other attempts to ensure school safety can at best offer marginal improvement.

Isolation and Uncertainty of Teacher

It was once thought to be a benefit of the profession that teachers work alone in their classrooms, behind closed doors. However, teacher isolation from each other and from administrators and other school staff, as well as from parents and the surrounding community, has become an increasing liability. The recent threats of privatisation, as well as salary cuts in several cities, are only the latest signs that teachers are isolated from their communities, without necessary public support. Unfortunately, the apparent loss of support for public schools comes at a time when new tasks—from "wanding" students with metal detectors, to talking to social workers and teaching socialisation skills—are being added to teachers' already stretched roster of daily responsibilities.

At the same time, a national uncertainty about how to handle potential conflicts between discipline, safety, and students' rights has made teachers unsure about what parents and the larger society want them to do. Can lockers be searched for weapons without giving students sufficient warning? Is it fair to wand only "suspicious-looking" students and not others? Do students have a right, as some claim, to carry weapons for their own defence? All these pressures have made many urban teachers feel overworked, stressed, and burned out.

A cynicism mirroring that of their students is prevalent among those who can see no way out. As a teacher commented, "You have people who have been in these dilapidated buildings for years, asking for help and getting empty promises. They just give up—throw up their hands and say, 'All I can do is deal with what I've got in front of me. Don't ask me to do anything more.'" Despite their acute concerns for safety, few teachers feel at ease in the increasingly garrison atmosphere of inner-city public schools. Rather than offering reassurance, metal detectors and other mechanical devices, as well as security forces, are seen as providing a false sense of safety, if not a harsh symbol of the failure to create safe schools.

In fact, finding weapons on students is relatively rare. In one typical case, a search of over 3,000 students yielded two weapons. This low rate of interception is partly because even the most sophisticated devices cannot catch all weapons entering a school. Unlike an airport, it is nearly impossible to secure every entrance to a school; those few students intent on bringing in weapons are inevitably a step ahead of the security devices, which means that enforcement activities alone cannot create a safe school.

Finally, metal detectors, wands, and security forces with guns, handcuffs, and other equipment, are taking large chunks out of already stretched urban education budgets, even as they increase, rather than alleviate, tension in schools. The garrison atmosphere is exacerbating tensions between students and school staff, who are forced to serve in policing roles. Conflicts are also emerging between teachers, who want to build trust for learning, and the security staff, whose orientation is toward control and arrests. Similarly, friction is surfacing between administrators, whose role is to promote the school and its students, and security forces, who often have no allegiance to the school but are anxious to increase their counts of weapons, violent incidents, and arrests.

While security forces and mechanical devices are the most obvious and controversial responses to school violence, many schools have also taken advantage of special federal, state, and local money aimed at anti-violence programming. Unfortunately, there have been several serious problems with these funds.

First, whether directed to preventing dropouts, drugs, or violence, the money has tended to be restricted to extremely narrow and fragmented programming. Despite growing evidence, for example, that new or well-kept school buildings increase student performance and morale, anti-drug or violence money can never be used for building repairs. Similarly, the high unemployment rates in inner-cities have been repeatedly linked to crime and violence, yet job programmes are rarely part of anti-violence measures. Even extra-curricular activities, after-school centres or sports programming, which are such a direct means of keeping students out of harm's way, rarely meet the tight programming restrictions of these funds. This missed opportunity is particularly sad, since student participation in sports and extra-curricular activities has decreased in the past decade.

Second, anti-violence and other youth assistance programmes in schools have tended to be isolated from, and to duplicate, programming in other public agencies. In fact, competition for money in the context of overlapping services has created a territoriality and fear of sharing knowledge and resources among educators, and social service and other professionals. In this environment of competition and suspicion, teachers are rarely an active part of either programme planning, or decisions about the needs of an individual student. Instead, they tend to be left out of the loop entirely, or to be given only limited and pre-designed tasks.

Strategies for Constructing Safer Schools

The web of educational and societal problems described above are deep and difficult to solve. Certainly, money is needed to repair schools and neighbourhoods and to create jobs for youth. It has also become obvious, however, that the ways in which schools and other public agencies approach social problems must change.

Educators and other professionals must make wider connections, both in human and conceptual terms. Although few believe that educational efforts, isolated from the surrounding society, can solve the problem of violence inside schools, there is widespread faith that some changes can make a difference. Moreover, a number of strategies being tried in schools around the country have improved safety and harmony.

Recruitment and Training of Teachers

School violence has given new urgency to improving the recruitment and training of teachers, particularly those entering urban schools. It is not enough for recruitment to focus only on finding role models—that is, teachers of the same race/ethnicity as their students. To heal the alienation and hopelessness of urban students, teachers must be found who will live in the communities where they work, so they can help reweave the torn fabric of community between teachers, students and their parents.

At the same time, the complex nature of today's schools necessitates a wider vision of which school staff need job preparation. Training must go beyond teachers, administrators, counsellors, and other professionals. It must extend to all employees, including paraprofessionals, cafeteria staff, secretaries, custodians, and bus drivers. Finally, the content of training must be reshaped. Both immediate, in-service and long-term, pre-professional training are necessary:

In-service Training. All school staff need to know how to address the immediate problem of violence in classrooms, the cafeteria, the halls, and other school areas, including on school buses. How should an adult behave when a student has a gun? What are the most effective methods of diffusing potential conflict among students, or breaking up fights?

Pre-professional Training. The pre-professional training of teachers, counsellors, and administrators has to be expanded to include more social analyses, so that prospective educators develop a deeper understanding of the issues that impinge on violence: poverty, the media, gun control, the changing economy and joblessness, and parenting. In addition, school staff needs to be better prepared to teach socialisation skills and nonviolent conflict mediation. Finally, because the traditional isolation of professionals from one another is no longer tenable, school staff must be trained to work cooperatively with each other, as well as with professionals outside the school.

Although coercive methods may stop violence in the short run, too often they create negative emotions that start their own cycle of undesirable behaviours. An alternate approach, which develops self-respect and self-discipline in students and positive working relationships, is obviously better for both students and adults, and for the climate of the school. Although small, unrelated programmes rarely make much of a difference, school-wide interventions that have general support can be helpful. For example, a number of schools have begun to focus specifically on increasing students' self-esteem, as well as on building the socialisation skills that many middle-class students learn at home.

In some schools, teachers and students are asked to get to know each other, including their strengths, likes, dislikes, humour, and triggers. The object is to come to a consensus about goals, and to create an ownership of, and engagement in, the daily activities of both teachers and students. Several elementary schools are teaching students simple skills, such as how to greet each other and interact with each other in respectful ways. Finding alternatives to cross-sex and same-sex teasing is key, for teasing starts early and leads to goading, heckling, and other forms of aggression, which can be quite dangerous by secondary school. Finally, both elementary and secondary schools across the country are teaching students, parents, and school staff the many benefits and methods of resolving conflict nonviolently, including peer mediation and de-escalation skills.

Role of Counsellors

Although the best way to prevent school violence is to change how everyone relates to each other, a number of schools are achieving good results by adding guidance counsellors and giving counsellors new roles. At least as important as intervening in crises and talking to students in the aftermath of violence is classroom teaching by counsellors. There, counsellors generate group work and developmentally oriented activities to improve the way students feel about themselves and interact with each other, particularly during stress or conflict.

Some counsellors are also working with cafeteria staff, bus drivers, and other support staff, as well as with parents. The goal is to give everyone involved in the school the same skills, language, and terminology for handling stress and conflict—to create an environment that is consistently nonviolent and nurturing.

Influence of Parents

Head Start, special education, and other compensatory education programmes have long involved parents in their children's schooling. However, the growing number of "children with children" and other unprepared or overburdened parents puts new pressure on urban schools to support families, as well as teach parenting skills. Activities range from grandparent hotlines to programmes that bring parents and junior high students together to learn parenting skills. In all, the point is to help parents and guardians become aware of the parenting skills they possess; enhance their skills; and expand parents' choices in their guiding, teaching, and disciplinary roles. A number of schools are also working directly to bring parents into the school.

In some, community facilitators work with parents to make them more comfortable with schools. In others, classes are held on a four-day schedule; on the fifth day, the parents and the students come to school together to participate in activities. A special literacy programmes allows parents and students to learn together. And some schools are creating "half-way houses" just outside the school, where school employees, community volunteers, parent facilitators, and others all can come. There, without the fear of authority, parents can talk more freely about the needs of their children and obtain appropriate services.

Treatment for Victims

Students who have witnessed or been involved in violence suffer from post traumatic stress, which can include anxiety, fear, emotional constriction, attention difficulties, and sleeplessness. Thus, just as victims need counselling when they leave the emergency room, students who were bystanders to the violence need carefully led discussions to help them with their confusion, grief, and anger. Some schools have instituted first offender programmes, which usually involve four- or five-day training sessions for one parent as well as the student.

Unfortunately, these programmes have limited benefits, since many students involved in offences have deeper problems, and need more serious help. However, schools are creating quite useful programmes for students who have been suspended for violence. For example, the student and parent or guardian may be asked to sign a contract agreeing to joint counselling, as well as to tutoring for the youth. Then once the student returns to school, the student and parent make a one-year commitment to continue the counselling and the tutoring, and to train in mediation and conflict resolution skills.

Simply stated, a safe school is a place where students can receive a high quality education without the threat of violence. A number of schools are developing plans and strategies to implement safe schools. These plans work best when they are generated not only by school staff, but also by parents and representatives from community groups and agencies. Although every school's plan for a "safe school" looks different, the key is developing a consensus about what everyone wants the school to be like, and the rules that everyone is willing to uphold to make this happen.

School violence is placing new pressures on schools to reach out to police, gang intervention workers, mental health workers, social service workers, clergy, and the business community. In a city with a large tourist business, close ties to the business community have resulted in guarantees that all the culinary arts programme students in the vocational school will receive jobs upon graduation. In another city, parents bringing their children into an elementary school have the option of filling out a form that is entered into the computers of all the public health agencies. Though this raises privacy issues, creating joint centres of information can enhance efficiency for both parents and professionals. There are several advantages to strategies that connect jobs and services through the school.

First, since resources need to be where the students and their parents are, schools are a natural place to consolidate services.

Second, finding other agencies that provide services enables schools to put their own money back into education, where it belongs.

And third, since violence is not a school problem—it is a community and societal problem—its solution has to draw in a wider circle of participation.

Finally, whatever the specific strategy, there is a need to bring back a communal feeling to the schools, and once again to root the schools in their communities. To do this, students, school staff, parents, neighbours, and other interested citizens all have to become part of the fabric of the schools—stakeholders in its future and in the future of its students.

13

Crisis Management in the Schools

Suicide and sudden loss among student populations has become a major concern for school counsellors, teachers, parents and helping professionals. Classmates, parents, teachers, and relatives experience both the direct implications of a student's death and the residual long-term effects of a significant loss. The devastating feelings of loss at a young age can be a traumatic experience for schools. Inherently, personal loss or threat of loss also increases a person's suicide risk. Peers of adolescents who attempted suicide are vulnerable because suicide is higher:

- among persons with unstable social relationships;
- when a population is self-contained (as in school-as-community and school-as-institution);
- when imitative behaviour is common;
- when the element of bravado exists; and
- when the act is sure to be noticed.

Balk further identified acute emotional responses of students after the death of a peer. He revealed that while peer support and chances to talk with friends about the death at such a time of loss were important aids in coping with death, many peers feel uncomfortable talking about death. They frequently avoid the survivors to decrease their discomfort of not knowing what to say or how to say it. Balk maintained that young people sometimes hide their feelings of grief because such feelings often are not considered acceptable in public, and as a result, adolescents are often confused about the source of their recurring grief reactions.

The reactions of survivors who have experienced a suicide or sudden loss are likely to be complex, but typically include some or all of the following behavioural characteristics: denial, anger, blaming, shame, guilt, fear, intellectualisation, or hostility. Stanford and Hunt further suggested the need for direct intervention in schools with survivors. Shneidman noted that when a death occurs, particularly of an unexpected nature, there is no pattern of behaviour to draw upon, and confusion results.

Teachers also need help in understanding and handling young people's normal, yet often inappropriate, reactions to death. Young people often take clues as to how to react from the adults around them more than from the event itself. A paramount need is for counsellors, educators and other support personnel to process the emotional needs of survivors. Intervention to enhance coping skills could ultimately prevent future suicides, or related self-destructive behaviour.

When a young person commits suicide, or is the survivor of any kind of tragic death, the school counsellor is confronted immediately with a number of serious problems:

- Verifying what happened,
- Containing the information,
- Protecting the privacy of the family,
- Helping students cope with the death,

- Communicating beyond the school,
- Seeking resources in the community,
- Dealing with parents, and
- Minimising the possibility that other students may imitate the behaviour and take their own lives.

The first 48 hours following a student's suicide or tragic death are crucial. The specific things for a counsellor and his or her staff to do during the first 48 hours are listed below:

- Verify the death. Meet or call the family; share with family what school and staff plans to do; protect the family's right to privacy, but also share the critical survivor needs of students and staff.
- Convene School Crisis Management Team.
- Meet with faculty to provide accurate information and to implement school's crisis management plan.
- Designate a person to serve as a case manager.
- Call on city-wide crisis management teams or support services if needed.
- Identify staff member(s) who will follow the deceased student's class schedule to meet with teachers and classmates and to work the hallways following the crisis.
- Make counsellors and/or support staff available to students.
- Identify students about whom faculty and staff are concerned.
- Provide rooms for students to meet in small groups.

Following are some questions must be consider after a crisis due to suicide and sudden death.

- How and when should the staff be informed?
- Is there a clearly defined phone tree in place?
- How and when should the students be informed?
- What specific information will be shared about the tragedy with the teachers and staff?
- How will the school protect the family's privacy?
- Who is the spokesperson for the school and what information will be released to the media?
- What will staff members be told to say if contacted by the media?
- How should the personal possessions of the student be handled?
- If feeder schools are affected by the crisis, how should they be included in the overall postvention efforts?
- Will you have a "care center" for those students who are upset?
- Where will the "care center" be located?
- Who will supervise the "care center"?
- How will students be identified to come to the "care center"?
- How many days will the "care center" be in existence?
- What available staff will you utilise city-wide?
- How will teachers, who are emotionally upset, be assisted?

Mourning and Grief Process

Accepting the reality of the loss and confronting the fact that the person is dead are two of the most important initial tasks of mourning. The early denial and avoidance is quickly replaced by the realisation of the loss and it is necessary to feel the pain of the loss and work through the grief process.

The grief process includes adjusting to an environment in which the deceased is missing. Survivors must face the loss of the many roles the deceased person filled in their life (e.g., classmate, team member, close friend). Students need to recognise that symptoms such as startle reactions, restlessness, agitation, sleeplessness, depression and anxiety are typical intense reactions to a traumatic experience such as death. Also essential is coming to terms with the anger one often feels toward

(1) the person who has died,

(2) oneself, and

(3) others.

A final task of mourning is to redirect the belief that one should have somehow prevented the death.

Treatment for Adolescents

- Allow regression and dependency.
- Realise their lack of life experience in handling trauma.
- Allow expression of feelings such as sorrow, hostility, and guilt.
- Encourage discussion.
- Allow for fluctuations in maturity level.

– Watch for emergence of unfinished business or unresolved conflicts of the past.

– Answer questions and provide factual information.

– Correct distortions.

– Avoid power struggles with adolescents.

– Focus on strengths and constructive adaptive behaviours.

– Address conscious as well as unconscious guilt.

– Identify and help resolve adolescents' sense of powerlessness.

14

Safety Counselling

In ensuring school safety, the courts have sought to balance students' constitutional rights with the need for safety and freedom from violence in the schools. At present, the balance is thoroughly tilted towards efforts to effect tough safety and drug policies in the schools and against any extension of the current scant constitutional rights students enjoy. As the preoccupation with drugs and gang paraphernalia in the schoolhouse has escalated, school searches of students and seizures of their property in accord with the Fourth Amendment comprise a cutting edge issue for the courts and school authorities.

Over several decades, in a series of cases involving public school students, the U.S. Supreme Court and state courts have very gingerly both bestowed and limited Fourth Amendment rights. These cases suggest that the delicate balance between students, rights and school safety procedures is strongly tilting towards the rights of school authorities to proactively isolate and reduce perceived causes of school violence. Starting in 1968 and culminating in 1984, the law of the land concerning the status of students vis-a-vis school authorities shifted to a more constitutional basis.

Prior to that time, student-school rights were defined by the common law doctrine of "in loco parentis, which for centuries posited that school officials had the "right, duty, and responsibility to act in the place of a parent. Their right to act included the exercise of many parental powers, such as the right to search students for illegal items, or for those items merely considered as contraband under state or local law or school district policies, without the warrant or probable cause mandated for all other citizens under the Fourth Amendment. The doctrine of in loco parentis began crumbling in 1968, when Tinker v. Des Moines Independent School District found for the first time that constitutional rights—in this case, the First Amendment right to wear a black armband in school as symbolic speech in protest against the Vietnam War—were applicable to students.

In landmark language that has been repeatedly cited, if not always upheld, the court said, "It can hardly be argued that either students or teachers shed their constitutional rights to freedom of speech or expression at the schoolhouse gate". Tinker left unanswered the question of whether Fourth Amendment protections against unreasonable searches and seizures applied to students when searched by school authorities, and if so, with what restrictions, if any. It was not resolved until 1985, in New Jersey v. T.L.O..

In that case, an assistant vice principal opened and searched the purse of T.L.O. (as the student involved was identified to protect her identity), after she had been accused of violating the school's policy of smoking a cigarette on high school property. His search disclosed not only a pack of cigarettes but also rolling papers associated with marijuana use, marijuana, a pipe, plastic bags, a large sum of money, a list of students who owed T.L.O. money, and two letters that involved her in dealing marijuana. When she was arrested on drug charges, she claimed that the evidence found in her purse should be suppressed as the fruits of an unreasonable search and seizure.

The court decided in [the case of] T.L.O. that students subjected to school searches are, in fact, citizens covered by the Fourth Amendment. Also, for the first time, the court considered school officials, when acting in furtherance of publicly mandated educational and disciplinary policies, far more akin to government agents—the very subject of Fourth Amendment restrictions—than to parental surrogates who, under the doctrine of in loco parentis, were free from constitutional restraints. The final question considered by the court was whether the search was reasonable, as guaranteed by the Fourth Amendment.

The Amendment requires a warrant and probable cause before a search is considered reasonable, although there are several exceptions to the imposition of that formulaic and high standard. The T.L.O. court carved out another such exception to the usual standard; it found that the Fourth Amendment's requirement of reasonableness was met if school authorities acted without a warrant, but with "reasonable grounds for suspecting that the search will turn up evidence that the student has violated or is violating either the law or the rules of the school.

Such a search will be permissible in its scope when the measures adopted are reasonably related to the objectives of the search and are not excessively intrusive in light of the age and sex of the student and the nature of the infraction". Thus the "reasonable suspicion" standard was definitively asserted. It permitted school authorities to lawfully search students upon meeting its two-pronged test: the search must be (1) reasonable in inception, and (2) reasonable in scope. Some recent search cases in which the two-pronged "reasonableness test" was successfully applied include these:

- A school dance monitor, who, upon seeing that some students were inebriated, in contravention of school policy, took them to a private office and asked them to blow on her face.
- Upon hearing an unusual thud when a student threw his bag onto a metal cabinet, a security guard rubbed his hand along the bag to feel for a gun.
- Upon a student's report to a guidance counsellor that another student possessed an illicit drug, the administrator searched the latter student's book bag, because the administrator also had knowledge that the student had been previously disciplined for possession of a controlled substance.

The case law on student search and seizure has yielded a few other useful factors to consider when conducting a search to ensure that it is reasonable at the inception and in scope. They include the student's age, history, and school record; the seriousness and pervasiveness as a school problem of the suspected infraction or crime; the urgency that required the search without delay; the school official's prior experience with the student; and the evidentiary value and reliability of the information used to justify the search.

What cannot and will not be condoned by the courts are searches that are performed with malicious intent to deprive students of their rights, those where school officials know or should have known that their actions violated students' rights, those that are capricious or discriminatory, and those that do not closely follow school search policies. The T.L.O. rule and its progeny have been applied to the rights of school authorities to engage in the following acts:

- Search students' school lockers to look for contraband or illegal materials.
- Search a student's car in the school parking lot.
- Organise searches by drug-sniffing dogs or metal detector machines.
- Perform a visual or manual body cavity search.

Drug Testing Law

As contentious as Fourth Amendment issues have been, the lessons of the T.L.O. case were not substantially reviewed until the courts assessed the issue of mandatory and voluntary drug testing. Until 1995, the short answer to the question of whether schools could mandate all or a class of students to submit to blood or urine tests for drugs could be clearly answered: "no". Such testing was seen as a violation of students' reasonable expectation of privacy, and repugnant not only to the U.S. Constitution, but also to the nation's common sense of students' integrity. The courts did, however, make a distinction between mandatory and voluntary drug testing, with the latter subject to no Fourth Amendment protections, as it is based upon consent.

That distinction blurs, though, when the tests are used as a precondition for school enrolment or for participation in extracurricular activities. Until June 27, 1995, the courts were split on drug testing as a precondition for participating in extracurricular activities, with some courts approving it exactly because these activities are voluntary.

Case Law Trends

The citation of Vernonia has served as the precedent for

several constitutional decisions on the Federal district court or circuit court of appeals levels during the few years since its issuance. Stigile v. Clinton found a strong governmental interest in permitting random drug testing of high school athletes, when such testing is "undertaken in furtherance of the government's responsibilities, under a public school system, as guardian and tutor of children, entrusted to its care." Thompson v. Carthage School District permitted the generalised search of all males in the sixth through twelfth grades in an Arkansas school district that required them to empty their pockets and to submit to a "pat-down" for weapons by school authorities.

The Thompson court applied T.L.O.'s two-pronged "reasonable test" and then applied the lessons of Vernonia. It found that Vernonia—which established that random drug testing in the absence of individualised suspicion, was "reasonable," and that even the significant privacy invasion of a urinalysis was justified by the important government interest, as students' "reasonable guardian and tutor" in reducing drug abuse by student athletes—could buttress the court's rationale in permitting the invasive "pat-down" and emptying of pockets.

In Wallace by Wallace v. Batavia School District, the court cited Vernonia when it permitted as a reasonable seizure a teacher's grabbing a high school student's wrists and elbow and escorting her out of the classroom, after observing the student participate in a screaming match with another student and then threaten that student with physical violence. The finding of "reasonableness" was based upon Vernonia's dictum that the nature of students' "rights is what is appropriate for children in school."

Cheema v. Thompson extended the previously abandoned legal theory of schools' functioning in loco parentis. The court noted that Vernonia held that for many purposes "school authorities act in loco parentis" when it decided, on other grounds, that Sikh students in California cannot be forced to utterly abandon their possession of religiously mandated ceremonial knives or cease attending public elementary school. After Cheema, it could be posited that there are still legal grounds to argue that school authorities are endowed with parental rights when assuring students' safety and drug-free status, and that students' constitutional protections are subservient to those parental rights.

15
Fitness Counselling

The various dimensions of wellness among school children are an important aspect of professional counselling. Children participating in aerobic exercises can avoid many health problems. The increase in body fat is responsible for reduced cardiovascular capacity which in turn limits a child's ability to resist coronary heart disease. In addition, a lack of physical activity accounts for a host of diseases including hypertension, diabetes, impaired tolerance for heat, and various psychological disorders.

Exercise regimens that begin at a young age are more effective in promoting longevity and health than those begun later in life. As children become older, there is a strong tendency for them to participate less in physical activity. The drop in such participation between the ages of twelve and eighteen is dramatic.

Collaboration between school counsellors and physical education teachers is also presented. Some promising studies have shown that school children can enhance their psychological as well as physical functioning after participating in fitness programmes that include aerobic running. All of the aerobic exercises have the potential to assist in promoting physical and psychological health, however, children and adolescents will find running activities to be the most accessible aerobic exercise in terms of skills development, costs, and availability.

Children who have experienced aerobic improvements have realised various degrees of self-esteem enhancement. Hyperactive, learning disabled, and behaviourally handicapped children have been found to internally control behaviours that were previously externally controlled following participation in running programmes. Running has even been found to be equivalent to low dosages of stimulants in treating hyperkinetic behaviour among children.

Relatedly, psychotropic medications have been reduced in emotionally handicapped children who run regularly. A downward trend has been reported in the depressive mood scores of hyperactive children following a 10-week running programme. Children with developmental problems also have increased completion of written tasks and reduced their degree of talking out in class as a result of participating in running programmes. In addition, improvements in academic learning and creative thinking have been associated with running exercise.

Children should be taught aerobic exercises at school that are prevention and protection oriented. Participating in school running programmes can influence the major systems of their bodies, reduce the risk of coronary heart disease, improve tolerance for stress, and promote wellness. Moreover, children who become physically fit are more likely to exert control over health risks and avoid behaviour that is counterproductive to good health.

In addition, children considered for adjunctive running programmes in the schools should obtain a physical examination prior to participation. This should assist in ruling-out any medical contraindications such as childhood rheumatic fever and asthma. Children prone to physical injury, foot abnormalities, and/or joint difficulties should be thoroughly assessed before consideration for a running programme.

Knowledgeable school counsellors, collaborating with physical education teachers, should utilise psychophysiological interventions whenever appropriate. Aerobic running programmes need to be thoughtfully designed in collaboration with physical education teachers. This will ensure that running programmes are individualised to meet the needs of the child's presenting issues. The flexibility of the programme is an important consideration due to children having varying initial levels of fitness.

Once the physical education component is considered, school counsellors and physical education teachers can plan running activities for children with particular problems. For example, a child with behavioural and/or emotional problems may be assigned to supervised running the first 20 minutes of the school day followed by a brief contact with the school counsellor. Similarly, a self-contained classroom with hyperkinetic children could engage in a group running activity and subsequent group discussion focused on running accomplishments. Thus, a self-esteem enhancement as well as a calming effect could occur.

Hinkle and Tuckman's article on managing children's running programmes is helpful for school counsellors. These authors' systematic running programmes within the schools have improved fitness levels in elementary and middle school students. They offer a simple method to measure aerobic capacity and discuss the management of structured running programmes for school children. In addition, group running formats, medical issues, and behaviour reinforcement are presented.

16

Guidance for Parents

The earlier fathers became involved with their children's learning and socialisation, the better. For example, Yarrow et al. observed 6- to 12-month-old infants separately with mothers and fathers at home and in a laboratory setting. They found that in 6-month-old infants, parental attention and sensory stimulation, especially of mothers, was associated with infant persistence. At 12 months of age, significant results were found only in relation to paternal stimulation and boys' persistence at practicing sensorimotor activities.

Clarke-Stewart observed fathers, mothers, and children 15, 20, and 30 months of age, at home in unstructured and semi-structured situations. She found that the intellectual skills of 15- to 30-month-olds were significantly related to the fathers' engagement in unstructured play, fathers' positive rating of children, the amount fathers and children interacted, and fathers' aspirations for children's independence as measured on an age-expected questionnaire.

Development of Early Literacy

In areas such as children's early reading, Gadsden and

Bowman, in a critical review of research on father involvement in children's education and schooling, conclude that fathers' participation in literacy activities, the barriers that parents face as a result of low literacy, and their perceptions of the role that they can play in their children's literacy development may affect children's preparedness for school. These factors also may influence the direct and subtle messages that fathers send to their children about the value, achievability, and power associated with literacy, schooling, and knowledge.

Although mothers' education historically has been used as the primary predictor of children's achievement, educational research increasingly is examining the effect of father-child interaction on children's early learning, particularly among fathers with low incomes. In a study of 50 low-income African American fathers participating in fatherhood programmes, Gadsden et al. examined fathers' beliefs regarding the valuing, uses, and problems of literacy learning for themselves and in relation to their children's early schooling.

Fathers' accounts suggested that many fathers felt challenged by the expectations attached to parenting roles-a challenge that was exacerbated by their own limited formal literacy capacities and their desire to support their children's early literacy development. In addition, fathers' beliefs about their children's educational success and future possibilities were ambivalent, often contraindicated their practices, and sometimes were at odds with their self-perceptions of facilitating children's literacy achievement. The researchers remind us that low-income African American fathers are a diverse group, not only in their literacy abilities, literacy experiences, literacy preparation, and goals for their children, but also in their family relationships and family resources. These and other studies suggest that a father's ability to support his child's learning affects the child's engagement with books and schooling.

Fathers (and mothers) who have limited schooling as well as low reading and writing abilities have difficulty participating in school-related activities requiring high levels of literacy. However, these parents have high hopes for their children and depend on programmes to ensure that their children will become competent learners. Research suggests that even when fathers have limited schooling, their involvement in children's schools and school lives is a powerful factor in children's academic achievement. Nord, Brimhall, and West analysed data from the 1996 National Household Education Survey (NHES) to compare the involvement of nonresident and married fathers in school activities of kindergarten to 12th-grade students.

Married and nonresident fathers' involvement in four types of school activities during the school year were examined-attending a general school meeting, attending a class or school event, attending a parent-teacher conference, and volunteering. Involvement was defined as low if fathers did none or one of the four activities during the school year, moderate if they did two activities, and high if they did three or four activities. Fathers in two-parent families and nonresident fathers who were moderately or highly involved in their children's school had children who were significantly more likely than children with less involved fathers to receive mostly high marks, enjoy school, and never repeat a grade.

Research that examines the extent to which fathers are involved with their children's schools has generally shown that fathers are less involved than mothers in all types of school activities. In particular, Nord, Brimhall, and West found that fathers with less than a high school education were much less likely to be involved in their children's schools than fathers with higher levels of education. Although nonresident fathers were found to be substantially less involved with their children's school than fathers residing with their children, Nord, Brimhall, and West indicated that the involvement of nonresidential fathers was in no way trivial.

Grolnick and Slowiaczek examined whether the motivational resources (e.g., self-regulation, perceived competence, and control understanding) of 300 11- to 14-year-old children mediate between three types of paternal involvement (e.g., behaviour with regard to school, the child's perception of the parent's affective and personal availability, and exposure of the child to intellectual and cognitive activities) and school performance (e.g., grades). They reported that for fathers two of the involvement factors (behaviour and intellectual/cultural activities) both uniquely influenced perceived competence and indirectly influenced school performance. In a recent study of Head Start children, Fagan and Iglesias used a nonequivalent control group design to assess whether participation in a Head Start based father involvement intervention influenced child outcomes (e.g., early academic readiness in reading and mathematics, social skills, and problem behaviours).

The intervention involved adapting traditional Head Start parent involvement activities (e.g., volunteering, weekly Fathers' Day programmes, father sensitivity training with staff, monthly support groups for fathers, and father-child recreational activities). Three levels of father participation (e.g., low, adequate, and high) were measured. Fagan and Iglesias report a positive association between high-level participation in a father involvement project and change in children's mathematics readiness scores. Early literacy development is a significant part of preparing children to achieve academically.

Children's early literacy is one of the areas to show the most promise in engaging fathers. Although empirical studies in this area are few, the applied activities suggested in Young Children and other publications demonstrate how fathers can be invited to engage in basic literacy activities. Literacy researchers have identified a range of early literacy behaviours that are associated with children's engagement with texts and success in reading:

- Oral language development, which includes book reading
- Phonemic awareness activities
- Exposure to the alphabet

In more expansive definitions of literacy, a parent's engagement is not limited specifically to reading and writing but encompasses a range of cognitive and social learning. As we know, young children acquire phonemic awareness through nursery rhymes, jingles, poetry, and books that contain words with rhymes and alliteration. Book reading, one of the most important activities in providing a context for language development, is an essential component of an effective preschool curriculum. It is intimately tied to language development, helps children to develop phonemic awareness and mastery of the concepts of print, and can be used to engage fathers with the programme and at home.

Children's development of early literacy begins at birth and relies on a range of environmental stimuli. Fathers can ensure that their children are exposed to the best environmental stimuli by participating at home and in early childhood education settings, which are often children's first significant experience outside of the family. In this way, fathers can be supported as they foster optimal early childhood experiences through which their children can develop cognitive abilities. For example, they can tell stories, read and select books with their children, and learn how to use appropriate visual and cognitive cues.

Early childhood educators can introduce fathers to approaches that provide opportunities for children to scribble and write, learn new vocabulary, identify letters and important words such as their names, and utilise relevant print within and outside the household (e.g., the brand names on milk cartons and street signs). They can also encourage fathers to talk with their children, a critical but often under-rated parent-child activity. This type of support could be integrated within the context of a programme's family involvement practices or presented as a workshop that is followed up with activities involving both mothers and fathers.

Parents might be asked to maintain a portfolio of their children's efforts-that is, a folder of the child's best work-which both child and parent choose. This activity requires that parents follow through on helping their children with literacy tasks, acknowledge their role in their children's learning, and maintain a relationship with the programme. Fathers who do not live in the same household with their children can also use this activity as a tangible way to connect with them regularly around a shared activity of interest and demonstrate that they value literacy.

Parents who have low levels of English language and literacy skills can read aloud, recite rhymes, and sing songs to children in their home language. In these cases, early childhood educators can clarify how children's early literacy experiences in the home language support them as English-language learners. A father can describe what he is doing while engaging in household tasks and ask the child to predict what he might do next. Fathers might also create games that require reading, writing, and problem solving.

Family Counselling

Family counselling represents a distinctive alternative for resolving persistent problems in the schools. Family counselling training has a short history and re-training opportunities for school counsellors wanting to engage in family counselling have been limited. Family interventions by school counsellors can address a child's misbehaviour, making costly special placements unnecessary. Furthermore, school counsellors are in a unique position to appreciate the effectiveness of family counselling approaches with children.

For example, children can become symptomatic at school when a crisis occurs at home; these symptoms may then serve a systems function by getting help for the troubled family. Using this family systems approach, school counsellors can apply family counselling to solve a child's problems and assist the child's family in finding solutions to problems from a social context. Therefore, from a systemic perspective, dated cause-and-effect logic becomes meaningless when dealing with children in the schools.

After eliminating specific school causes for presenting problems, school counsellors should consider etiology that is based out of school. According to systems theory, when a child's problem persists, it is usually connected to the extended social unit or family. Therefore, it is best to solve the problem by including the school as well as the family in formulating a solution. This perspective suggests that a student's negative behaviour is connected to how the parents and other family members respond when the problem behaviour occurs.

It is important for the school/family counsellor to ask how the problem is maintained in the system? Idiosyncratic approaches to school problems have at times required inordinant amounts of time and resulted in little substantial improvement. However, school counsellors utilising family counselling within the school have reported successful interventions for brief periods of time when compared to lengthy individual counselling. If the problem is more complicated or requires long-term counselling, family interviews conducted by school counsellors can significantly aid in a referral to an outside community agency. If the family is referred outside the school, the school counsellor may even attend the first "extended family" session.

There has been limited family counselling training in school counselling programmes, resulting in little family counselling among school counsellors. However, this approach to helping children with difficulties is increasing. As a result, school counsellors re-training in family counselling will need to obtain support from school administrators. After support is established, training will ultimately require a paradigm shift for those counsellors previously trained in one-to-one, individualistic counselling. To utilise the family systems approach, the school counsellor will need to become more directive, less passive and neutral, and expand upon skills developed during training in individual counselling.

Effectively dealing with the transition from the role of helper to change agent also will be an important aspect of re-training. Such re-training should focus on elective study in family counselling that may include additional graduate courses, continuing education, and/or inservice training. Re-training in family counselling prepares a counsellor to work in a limited role with families. It may include introductory graduate courses in family counselling and subsequent supervised practice.

Disadvantages to this re-training format include limited preparation to deal with complex systems problems. However, advantages include "on the job" exposure to family counselling without extended training. In addition, becoming familiar with the literature in family counselling is essential to re-training. This should continue with a focus on family counselling skills and techniques. Since they typically have not learned sufficient techniques to begin effective family counselling, school counsellors will find readings about family counselling quite rewarding. It is also beneficial for school counsellors re-training in family counselling to form study groups and affiliate with professionals who specialise in family counselling.

Study groups can view and learn from videotapes of master counsellors in addition to their own family counselling. Role playing and consulting with each other regarding family cases will also be helpful. School counsellors can also seek out local family counsellors willing to provide consultation and/or supervision. Additionally, opportunities to do co-therapy with experienced family counsellors should be sought in order to develop specific competencies in family counselling.

Competencies in Family Counselling

Two primary skills for school counsellors doing brief family counselling in the schools are assessing the family's capacity to change and defining the key concepts of the problem within a social context. Assessment should minimally include obtaining new information which leads to hypothesis generation regarding the family. Identifying the family hierarchy in terms of "power" and knowing how and where family information flows also is important to family assessment.

Assessment should always include the family's understanding of the problem and the family's strengths, as well as what the family has done thus far to solve the problem. Eventually, family interventions within the school will include the development of a plan and a prescription that includes reframing problem behaviour and assigning homework tasks. School counsellors will need to acquire skills at establishing rapport with the family system, showing caring and concern, as well as sharing positive characteristics of the child with the family. Consulting with parents about their child and assisting with their understanding of child and adolescent behaviour also are important family counselling competencies.

Many parents need assistance with re-establishing their executive position as primary decision-makers within their family. Effective relationships between parents and grandparents and other extended family members also must be established. Parents frequently need help in establishing behavioural expectations and discipline for their children. Child behavioural problems that are a function of marital discord should also be identified and an appropriate referral made.

Retention

A child may be considered for retention if he or she has poor academic skills, is small in stature or the youngest in the grade, has moved or been absent frequently, does poorly on a prescreening assessment, or has limited English-language skills. In addition, a retained child is more likely to be male and to have minority status, a high activity level, low socioeconomic status, and parents who are unwilling or unable to intercede for the child.

Retention is also more commonly used in the primary grades. In a few cases, the teacher may feel that the child is capable of moving forward, but the parent may prefer that the child be retained. Since most schools have vague policies regarding retention, the decision typically falls to the classroom teacher.

Research from the Gesell Institute suggests that children benefit from careful developmental assessment and placement in the early grades. Some teachers and parents believe that appropriate placement encompasses retention and that certain children will benefit from the maturity gained from an extra year in the same grade. However, cumulative research on the effects of retention shows that the negative effects usually outweigh the positive effects. The National Association of School Psychologists (NASP) notes the following among the negative effects:

— Cost children do not "catch up" when held back.

— Although some retained students do better at first, these children often fall behind again in later grades.

— Students who are held back tend to get into trouble, dislike school, and feel badly about themselves more often than children who go on to the next grade.

In addition to the conclusions that NASP has drawn from the research, the weakened self-esteem that usually accompanies retention plays a role in how well the child may cope in the future. Research has shown that children view the thought of flunking a grade to be almost as stressful as the death of a parent or blindness. "Even more staggering is the fact that being held back twice makes dropping out of school a virtual certainty".

In view of the larger body of research on retention, the continued use of retention is one of the clearest examples of poor communication between research and practice. Professors Smith and Shepard at the University of Colorado found that teachers frequently exaggerated the perceived benefits of retention. They believed that retention in early grades prevented problems or the stigma of failure later on. But teachers lacked real feedback on how well students were doing as they moved through school.

Also, the practice of retention gives the appearance of a school's being accountable about a problem and enforcing standards but may neglect the underlying cause of a student's failure. There are also some philosophical differences among professional educators. Some teachers believe that children mature and develop school readiness along with physiological unfolding, while other teachers believe that any child of legal age is teachable if the programme is adapted to fit that child's individual needs. In one study, the teachers who leaned toward physiological readiness also leaned towards retention, while the other teachers were more likely to change their teaching methods to meet the individual child's needs.

Another difficulty for a teacher or parent, as he or she assesses the possibilities for the child, is the basic dilemma of choosing from the options that are available in their school or community. It is important for parents and teachers to become aware of some of the alternatives to retention. These include:

– Mixed-age classes. In this environment, students learn at their own rate and advance to the next stage when they have mastered the required skills without the restriction of grade-level labelling.

- Individualised instruction. This method is tailored to the individual student's style of learning.
- Tutoring. Through individual attention, students are helped in difficult academic areas throughout the year.
- Home assistance programmes. These programmes provide parents with structured specific information about ways to help their child academically with homework, sound study habits, or sound work habits.
- Smaller class size. Particularly in the primary years, small class size improves learning environments for all students.
- Seeking alternative educational settings. These may include summer school or after-school programmes that are learning laboratories with lots of opportunities for projects and a "hands on" approach to learning.
- Guidance counselling. In an advisor/advisee type of relationship, an "at-risk" student may be identified earlier and given consistent support throughout his or her school career.
- Delaying achievement testing that may lead to retention. Achievement testing may be useful for identifying weak areas in the school curriculum and possibly areas where the child needs additional support; however, it should not be taken out of context of other information and become the deciding factor for grade placement for a child.

When parents are faced with retention as an option for their child, they can:

- Make an effort to understand why the teacher is suggesting retention. Parents can ask to see examples of their child's work compared to the work of other children of the same age. If the teacher is concerned about the child's maturity or behaviour, parents can ask for specific examples of behaviour that cause concern.
- Keep the teacher informed about the parents' knowledge of the child. If the child was within the normal ranges of early developmental benchmarks, parents can let the teacher know. How does the child's school behaviour compare with his or her at-home behaviour? Are there similarities or large differences?
- Be aware of the stresses that may be affecting the child and keep the teacher informed. For example, if the family has a new baby in the house, or has recently moved, these life changes can affect the child's behaviour for a short period of time.
- At home, ask the child about homework and give him or her a quiet place to study.
- Be certain that the child eats nutritious meals, gets enough sleep, and stays healthy.
- Request assistance from other support staff in the school. The school psychologist, school counsellor, or special education staff may be able to evaluate the child and suggest an alternative intervention.

Some psychologists notes that retention is not as likely to be harmful when the student:

- lacks serious deficits in the year prior to retention;
- has positive self-esteem and good social skills;

– shows signs of difficulty in school because of lack of opportunity for instruction rather than lack of ability; or

– does not have serious social, emotional, or behavioural deficits.

If a child repeats a grade, parents should work with school personnel to be sure that their child has a significantly different experience during the retained year from the previous year and that the child is assessed and placed at the appropriate developmental level. Some options might include a classroom with a lower teacher-student ratio, a different curriculum, or a different approach to learning. It might also be beneficial to move the child to another school. If retention is chosen, then the extra year should not be just a repetition of the previous year, but it should be individualised in such a way that it contributes to the child's future success.

17

Guidance and the Effective Education

A new school of thought is emerging among educators and counsellors. Unlike the reform movement of the past decade, this new movement takes full account of students' personal needs in formulating educational goals. Proponents of this school of thought recognise the close relationship between students' academic development and their personal growth; accordingly, they are seeking to place guidance at the heart of the educational process.

Norm Gysbers' Comprehensive Guidance Programme Model, and Robert Myrick's Teacher Advisor Programme are both based on the idea that guidance is an integral part of a school's educational mission rather than an "ancillary" service peripheral to the curriculum. This idea in turn presupposes an enlightened humanistic conception of education, which recognises and validates the intrinsic dignity of every student, and which attends empathetically to students' personal and developmental needs. This conception forms the basis of William Purkey's Invitational Learning Model, a new paradigm for schooling that seeks to reconstitute the entire school setting—people, places, policies, programmes, and processes—so that every aspect of the school serves to "invite" students to learn by respecting them, encouraging them, and validating their unique importance and possibilities.

Comprehensive Guidance Programme Model

Since 1971, Norman C. Gysbers and his associates at the University of Missouri-Columbia have been developing, field-testing, refining, and implementing the Comprehensive Guidance Programme Model, an innovative, programme-based organisational plan that has been adopted by school districts throughout the nation. The foundation for the Model—the theoretical basis for identifying the guidance, knowledge, skills, and attitudes (competencies) that students need is called Life Career Development, defined as self-development over a person's life span through the integration of roles, settings, and events in a person's life. Accordingly, this Model emphasises three domains of human growth and development:

- Self-knowledge and interpersonal skills. Helping students to develop awareness and acceptance of themselves and others, and to develop personal standards and a sense of purpose in life.
- Life roles, settings, and events. Emphasising knowledge and understanding of the interrelatedness of various life roles.
- Life career planning. Appraising personal values as they relate to prospective life career plans and decisions.

The Comprehensive Guidance Programme Model consists of three structural foundations and four interactive programme components. The structural foundations—definition, rationale, and assumptions—emphasise the centrality of guidance to the total education programme, and define the relationship between guidance and other aspects of the curriculum. The four programme components delineate the major activities, and the roles and responsibilities of personnel involved in the guidance programme:

- Guidance curriculum, or structured classroom activities, organised around the three domains of student competencies;
- Individual planning, including activities designed to assist students in monitoring and understanding their own growth and development;
- Responsive services, such as information seeking, crisis counselling, and teacher/parent/specialist consultation; and
- System support, activities geared toward programme management and operations.

One principal rationale behind the Comprehensive Guidance Programme Model is to enable counsellors to regain control of their time on the job by allocating 100 percent of their time to the four programme components discussed above—guidance curriculum, individual planning, responsive services, and system support. The Comprehensive Guidance Programme Model is oriented above all toward student development; it is a programmematic framework which allows counsellors to devote their primary attention to guidance activities and structured group experiences for all students.

TEACHER ADVISOR PROGRAMME (TAP)

The assumption behind Robert D. Myrick's Teacher Advisor Programme (TAP) is that each student needs a friendly adult in the school who knows and cares about him or her in a personal way. The advisors help their advisees deal with the problems of growing up and getting the most out of school. A teacher-advisor is usually responsible for an advisee's cumulative folder, work folders, teacher-student conferences, parent conferences, group guidance experiences and follow-up on academic progress reports. Advisors also consult with other teachers, school counsellors, and support personnel about their advisees.

TAP is designed to provide an opportunity for all the students in a school to participate in a small and cohesive group of 15 to 25 peers led by a sensitive and caring teacher who promotes and monitors individual students' educational and developmental experiences as they progress through school. Teacher-advisors meet with their advisees on a regular basis through a "homeroom" or "homebase" group. This becomes, in effect, the students' home within the school, where they have a supportive teacher and group of peers with whom they can explore personal interests, goals, and concerns. The guidance curriculum varies from one school to another, but it generally addresses personal, social, and academic concerns.

Some of the personal and social skills addressed include getting acquainted, self-esteem, and time management. Academic topics might include policies and procedures from the school handbook and computing grade point averages. Career and educational planning topics include career exploration and choices, employability skills and the job market. Since many high school teachers have never had a guidance course and many are unsure of how to lead a group discussion with adolescents, teachers may need special preparation in how to work with their students and how to build guidance units for their groups.

Counsellors can therefore assist teachers in developing guidance units, or they can work together as a team in developing and delivering a guidance curriculum, with counsellors taking over homebase groups on occasion. It is important, therefore, to establish a cooperative and supportive relationship between teachers and counsellors so that they can define their respective roles and differentiate responsibilities. To enlist the support of a school's faculty for TAP and developmental guidance, it is essential that all teachers understand the philosophy of TAP and commit adequate time to it.

Counsellors should therefore provide a developmental guidance curriculum guide to establish guidance objectives and provide activities, but allow teachers to choose or discard suggested activities according to their needs. Since most teachers need more training in how to help students solve personal problems or get them working cooperatively in small groups, counsellors also may need to assist teachers in developing guidance and interpersonal skills. Administrative support and periodic evaluation are also essential.

Invitational Learning

The Invitational Learning concept, developed by William W. Purkey, offers a blueprint of what counsellors, teachers, principals, supervisors, superintendents, and others can do to enrich the physical and psychological environments of institutions and encourage the development of the people who live and work there. Invitational Learning is based on four value-based assumptions regarding the nature of people and their potential and the nature of professional helping:

– *Respect*: People are able, valuable, and responsible and should be treated accordingly;

– *Trust*: Education should be a collaborative, cooperative activity where process is as important as product;

– *Optimism*: People possess untapped potential in all areas of human endeavor; and

– *Intentionality*: Human potential can best be realised by places, policies, programmes, and processes that are specifically designed to invite development, and by people who are intentionally inviting with themselves and others, personally and professionally.

In a school or any other organisation, everything is connected to everything else. And so, in applying Invitational Learning, everything counts in creating an environment that invites individuals to reach their potential:

– *Places*: Creating an attractive and inviting physical setting is the easiest way to begin the process of incorporating the Invitational Learning concept into a school or other organisation.

– *Policies*: Professional counsellors can assist schools in developing policies that encourage student responsibility and participation rather than those that create pervasive anxiety, mistrust, and mindless conformity.

– *Programmes*: Programmes that incorporate the assumptions of Invitational Learning include incentive programmes such as peer counselling for dropout prevention, faculty mentoring, and other collaborative programmes where students, teachers, and counsellors all gain by helping and encouraging one another.

- *Processes*: How we teach or counsel and how we act while doing these things are far more important in the long run than what students or clients learn. Educators and counsellors in successful schools establish behavioural norms of collegiality, professional development, mutual assistance, and ongoing discussion of instruction and curricular improvements among themselves, and they cultivate attitudes of respect for all students and attention to their needs in all of their interactions.
- *People*: The daily interaction between teachers and students, counsellors and clients, and professionals amongst themselves, ultimately determines the success or failure of Invitational Learning. Counsellors and teachers who wish to employ Invitational Learning therefore need a sound knowledge of human development.

The goal of Invitational Learning is thus to provide an optimally inviting total environment, both for professional helpers themselves and for those with whom they work. In this respect, it is fully compatible with both the Comprehensive Guidance Programme Model and the Teacher Advisor Programme. All three approaches affirm the centrality of developmental guidance to the educational process, and all are predicated on mutual respect and human dignity—for counsellors, teachers, and students alike.

Ethical and Legal Issues

Ethical decisions are usually not clear-cut; they tend to be in the "gray areas" rather than in "black and white." Furthermore, the "right" answer in one situation is not necessarily the "right" answer in a similar case at another time. As society changes, the issues change; and, indeed, as counsellors change, their perspectives change. If we understand and accept the fact that ultimately counsellors will have to struggle with themselves to determine the appropriate action in each situation, then we realise the importance of ethical and legal awareness and sensitivity.

We then also understand the need for periodic re-examination of the issues throughout our professional lives. The importance of knowing the contents of professional codes of conduct and the purposes and limitations of such codes is essential to the understanding of ethical and legal issues in school counselling. Although detailed memorisation of the ethical codes is not required, school counsellors should have at least a basic understanding of their ethical responsibilities as defined in these documents.

The ethical standards of ASCA and the American Association for Counselling and Development (AACD) present school counsellors with the behaviours to which they should aspire and give general guidelines for addressing difficult issues. They do not, however, necessarily provide answers to the many specific dilemmas that practitioners will face. When the standards do not provide enough direction, counsellors are encouraged to consult with colleagues, professional experts, and perhaps their administrative supervisors before taking action. Almost all professionals, at some point in their career, suspect or become aware of a colleague's unethical behaviour.

School counsellors are obligated to address any conduct by a colleague that could cause harm to clients. Counsellors should:

(a) try to resolve the issue by confronting the colleague directly, if possible;

(b) report the behaviour to a superior, professional association, or credentialing authority if a direct confrontation is not possible or is not effective; and

(c) take steps to protect any vulnerable clients.

Confidentiality and Privileged Communication

Confidentiality and privileged communication are two related issues that school counsellors often confuse. Information clients relate to school counsellors should be kept confidential with the following general exceptions:

(a) the client is a danger to self or others;

(b) the client or parent requests that information be related to a third party; or,

(c) a court orders a counsellor to disclose information.

Although all school counsellors have a confidentiality responsibility, very few relationships with students are considered privileged. Privileged communication is granted only by statute and guarantees clients that a court cannot compel a counsellor to disclose information related in confidence. Such statutory privileges belong to clients rather than to counsellors, and most states do not grant privileged communication in school counselling relationships.

Legal Standards

Legal standards of practice are different from ethical

standards. Generally, legal standards are related to accepted professional practices in the community while ethical standards tend to be idealistic. Many schools have policies that differentiate between the rights of custodial and noncustodial parents, and school counsellors are often required to implement such policies. The law is clear that, barring a specific court order to the contrary, noncustodial parents have all rights regarding their children except the right to have custody of the children permanently in their homes. When federal legislation known as the 1978 Hatch Amendment was passed and revised regulations were issued in 1984, a great deal of misinterpretation occurred that inhibited the offering of school counselling services.

Eventually it was realised that the amendment's requirement of written parental consent for children to participate in certain school programmes covered only a narrow range of activities that were federally funded, were experimental in nature, and involved psychological tests or treatment. School counsellors often play a major role in administering the school's testing programme. School counsellors should provide expert advice to school policymakers regarding the appropriate use of tests. Counsellors should assist in evaluating each test to determine whether it:

(1) discriminates in any way against any segment of the school population,

(2) is valid and reliable,

(3) is appropriate for the purposes for which it is being used, and

(4) is necessary to achieve the school's objectives.

Moreover, the counsellor is responsible for interpreting test results for students in a clear and understandable manner.

The laws regarding abortions for minors are changing. Generally, school counsellors may discuss a student's decision of whether to seek an abortion with the student, but they should also encourage parental involvement when possible. Each case must be decided individually based on the facts as presented.

Group counselling presents ethical issues not found in individual interventions with clients. The advantages of a comprehensive group counselling programme are numerous; however, school counsellors who direct such programmes need to be familiar with potential ethical problems. Although group counselling in general presents special problems, providing group counselling for children introduces issues not found when working with adults. Although the ASCA Ethical Standards for School Counsellors does not directly address group counselling, some specific guidelines are found in the AACD Ethical Standards. The ASGW Ethical Guidelines for Group Counsellors provides additional direction.

Special Issues

Computers: School counselling offices are increasingly utilising computers and computer products. School counsellors have made attempts to understand and utilise this modern technology, but many counsellors are still unaware of the ethical issues involved in the use of computers. It is imperative that professional associations develop ethical standards regarding computer use. Moreover, the importance of direct counsellor-client contact in conjunction with the use of computers must be stressed.

Cultural diversity: School counsellors have a responsibility to provide services for all students, including those from other cultures. The counselling profession is a Western culture phenomenon; however, school counsellors constantly interact with families and children who speak languages other than English, adhere to values different from those of the counsellor, and conform to social expectations that may seem odd to the American school environment. The unique ethical issues involved in counselling multi-cultural populations need to be addressed.

Research: There is an increasing demand for school counsellors to engage in field-based research. Documenting programme effectiveness can do more to promote school counselling than all public relations efforts combined. But even if school counsellors never conduct research themselves, they need to know the rights of students involved in research projects, the responsibilities of researchers, and other research-related ethical issues.

Sexual intimacy: Perhaps the most pressing ethical problem in the counselling profession is sexual intimacy with clients. School counsellors are involved less often in sexual relationships with clients than are their colleagues who counsel adults. Nevertheless, clients, no matter what their age, often introduce sexual dimensions into the counselling relationship. Counsellors who are faced with sex and intimacy boundary issues in their professional counselling roles must respond in a manner that is consistent with ethical guidelines.

18

Challenges of Counselling

Challenge of Middle School Counselling

In middle schools, counsellors work with young people whose lives are in constant flux. Counsellors are called upon to plan programmes that make middle schools inviting places for young people to learn and grow. Middle school counselling programmes need to focus on preparing youngsters for the increased independence of life in high school that is typically accompanied by more social pressures and by increased stress.

Early adolescence is difficult for most youngsters, a time for challenging one's self and the ideas brought from childhood. It is the beginning of physical, emotional, social, and intellectual growth which brings excitement, delight, anxiety, and misunderstanding. The child, who in elementary school was obedient and academically motivated, may seem disrespectful and lazy in middle school. Early adolescence begins the transition from acceptance of adult direction to challenging authority and moving toward self direction.

The goal of middle school counsellors is to provide a blend of challenge and support that will promote identity development in early adolescence. Middle school students need the guidance and direction of effective counsellors to begin the major developmental task of adolescence which is to achieve a clear sense of self. The confusion that reigns in early adolescence creates a challenging climate for the young person and for those trying to help the youngster manage the difficulties associated with leaving childhood for a new stage of life. Counsellors implement various practical strategies to help middle school students move toward self understanding. These strategies include such activities as maintaining daily journals, group counselling, and developmental classroom programmes that offer young people opportunities for self exploration.

Problems of Family Relationship

As young people begin to seek their own identities, they face the challenge of leaving behind much of their early dependence on home and family. Parents and family members, however, should continue to provide structure and support during the difficult moments adolescents face in growing away from complete dependence on home. The so-called traditional family, however, has virtually disappeared in America. Divorce, single-parent homes, and step-families are a fact of life confronting youngsters.

In the climate of changing families, middle school counsellors need to be prepared to help youngsters and their parents understand one another and to work together in making the difficult choices that occur during adolescence. Middle school counsellors need to be especially aware of dysfunctional aspects of students' families in order to develop counselling strategies and guidance programmes that help young adolescents find themselves. Finally, and perhaps most importantly, counsellors need to be aware of cultural differences that students bring from their homes into middle school life and into the search for personal identities.

Early adolescence is a time of experimentation with new behaviours and of reliance on peers for guidance and direction. This combination can have devastating effects on young people's lives if it results in experimentation with alcohol and other drugs. Young people who begin to use alcohol and other mind altering substances during their middle school years may be especially prone to the problem of addiction later in adolescence and into adulthood. Most middle schools are not prepared to offer adequate prevention programmes to help youngsters challenge the social pressure to experiment with drugs.

In fact, the current status of drug education in schools throughout the United States is ambiguous at best. Theory-based prevention programmes that have been tested offer hope that drug abuse prevention programmes will improve. Assertiveness training programmes, for example, that are designed to help adolescents resist peer pressure, seem to offer middle school counsellors intriguing ideas for programme development. In addition, cognitive-development programmes that are intended to raise the psychological maturity of youngsters and improve their decision-making offer considerable hope for middle school counselling programmes. Middle school counsellors must understand the relationship between peer pressure and substance abuse and develop counselling strategies that are designed to help young adolescents deal with the pressures to use drugs.

Students in middle schools frequently complain about the stress they experience in their everyday lives. Typical adolescent complaints include "Everyone is watching for me to make mistakes" and "I never have any time for myself." Adults sometimes have a tendency to discount what adolescents say, believing that most of the stress youngsters experience will pass as maturation occurs. This lack of empathy on the part of adults may leave adolescents feeling misunderstood and alienated. Middle school counsellors must implement programmes that help young adolescents deal with many stressful circumstances. Desensitisation programmes that help in overcoming undue fears and relaxation programmes that attempt to relieve stress may help young adolescents develop confidence and hope for the future.

Problems of Physical Maturation

Physical maturation, and particularly sexual maturation, has significant effects on self-concept and social relationships during the middle school years. Most young adolescents dwell on how to make themselves more attractive and acceptable to their peers. One of the many difficult challenges for middle school counsellors is to attend to the concerns of adolescents about physical maturation and sexuality. Much has been written about adolescent sexuality, in particular, about topics such as friendship, sexual identity, and adolescent pregnancy.

Middle school counsellors must implement programmes that take into account the impact of physical and sexual maturation on students' lives. Counsellors should especially work to prepare adolescents to meet the challenging issues surrounding contraception and teen pregnancy.

Academic Challenges

Americans are becoming increasingly aware of the need for schools to promote academic excellence. Individuals in the business community and elsewhere complain that young people do not have the basic academic skills necessary for economic success in a competitive world. Governmental and private commissions have noted the high dropout rate in America's schools and the generally poor record of public schools in promoting academic excellence. Educators in the United States must account for the failure of schools to motivate young people to stay in school and to strive for high levels of academic achievement.

Middle school counsellors can contribute to schools' efforts at improving academic achievement among young teenagers. These days middle schoolers often have considerable freedom. Many are latchkey children who may choose what to do when they arrive home from a day at school. More often than not they choose leisure, neglecting their academic responsibilities.

Middle school counsellors should collaborate with teachers to implement programmes that help youngsters develop a reasonable "work ethic." Middle school counsellors can play an important role in helping young people see themselves as capable students who have the potential to realise academic success. Counsellors should take the lead in transforming low achieving and disruptive adolescents into model students.

Problems in Career Exploration

In the search for identity, young adolescents struggle not only with the question of "Who am I?" but also with the question "Who will I become?" The latter question is often answered in terms of future occupation.. Adolescents face an ever-changing world of work, a fact that is often neglected by overburdened middle school counsellors. The economic, political, and social changes that have brought women and minorities into the work force in large numbers have altered how youngsters must be prepared to enter the world of work.

Middle school counsellors have many opportunities to promote career development and career exploration among young people. It is especially important for young adolescents to learn the skills that will eventually help them achieve gainful employment. These skills include how to write a resume, how to fill out a job application, and how to interview effectively for a job. Middle school counsellors must be especially attentive to the special needs of exceptional students in the area of career exploration.

Challenge for Middle School Counsellors

The challenge for middle school counsellors is to develop focused programmes that meet specific developmental needs of young adolescents. Much like the students they serve, middle school counsellors must develop their own professional identities which are expressed in well defined and accountable school guidance programmes. Middle school counsellors cannot do everything. They are faced with issues such as dysfunctional families, substance abuse, teen pregnancy, teen suicide, sexual abuse, school dropouts, and numerous other difficult matters.

Counsellors, therefore, must set priorities and develop programmes to meet those priorities. Preventive and developmental programmes seem to be the most promising and cost-effective approaches to counselling with young adolescents in middle schools. Such programmes are likely to help young adolescents satisfactorily address the question, "Who am I?"

Building Leadership Skills

Girls had lower self-esteem than boys in middle school and the gender gap grew when girls transitioned from middle school to high school. Following are some explanations for the decline in self-esteem:

(1) girls are more negatively affected by experiences with failure than are boys. The sensitivity may limit their willingness to take risks for rewards or advanced opportunities;

(2) many girls experience a conflict between feminine goals and competitive achievements, resulting in increased anxiety in competitive situations;

(3) girls are confronted with societal and school structures that favour boys and with pressure to conform to gender roles that limit their exploration;

(4) girls are less satisfied with body image compared to boys, and this is compounded by pubertal changes; and

(5) girls are more likely to worry about their problems than boys and this tendency to worry puts girls at risk for depression.

Many middle schools offer interscholastic sports programmes for boys and girls. Students obtain a position on a team by competing in a "try-out," a new experience for most adolescents. Once selected, membership requires a commitment to compete in several games per week and practice for many hours daily. Sports teams for girls flourished as a result on the Title IX Educational Amendments of 1972 in U.S. Often referred to as Title IX, this federal law requires that almost all educational institutions provide educational opportunities to male and female students equitably, including their athletic programmes and offerings. Title IX seeks to level the playing field for both genders by mandating equal opportunities for participation.

LEADERSHIP

Dobosz and Beaty assert that leadership is the capability to guide others in the achievement of a common goal. Leadership characteristics consist of many personal qualities, including self-esteem, determination, organisational aptitude, focus, tolerance, decisiveness, self-discipline, charisma, time management, self-confidence, social competence, communicating a "vision," and sensitivity to the needs of others, among other qualities.

Middle school is the typical time for introduction to competitive sports for most adolescents. Thus, research collected at the "start gate" of middle school, if you will, will establish a benchmark of the impact of athletics on the development of leadership skills in girls. Yet, although Title IX has existed for over 30 years, limited research exists in examining this impact. Leadership skills that are instilled during early adolescence in girls evolve throughout adolescence and into adulthood. In fact, 80% of the female executives in Fortune 500 companies self-identified as having been athletes and/or "tomboys" in adolescence.

Membership on an athletic team is one avenue to acquire, assess, refine, and demonstrate leadership skills developmentally appropriate for middle school students. Participation in sports extends the nurturance of leadership by teaching girls to cooperate with their teammates and opponents as well as abide by the rules. Girls learn about taking turns, sharing play time, and valuing rules. A sense of fair play is instilled. They learn that without rules and regulations, the game would become unfair. If the players believe that everyone contributes to the team's success and feel as though they are being treated fairly, then each player's athletic ability and psychological stamina are maximised.

Athletic team membership enables girls to control and shape their lives, to feel empowered, in ways that other middle school girls feel that they cannot. Through participation in sports, girls tend to have higher levels of self-confidence, increased self-esteem, and lower levels of anxiety compared to non-athletic girls. Furthermore, the athlete's competitive spirit steers many team members to vie for student leadership positions such as team captain or to seek election to the student government.

Hart found that, in a sample of 108 girls in one middle school, girls on the soccer team held more leadership positions in school organisations and attained more leadership positions within the student council compared to non-athletic girls. Hart concluded that for the middle school-aged female athletes, confidence and empowerment are acquired through competitive sports and school leadership.

Learning effective time management is a major step towards leadership development for the middle school female athlete. She must learn early that time is finite, that she must set priorities, and that she must sacrifice experiences enjoyed by her peers. She must manage an athletic schedule, fulfil academic and extracurricular demands, participate in family activities and responsibilities, and attend to personal needs during the after-school hours. The mastery of time management, setting priorities, and multitasking are early stepping-stones to leadership.

The effects of self-esteem in student athletes and non-athletes have been investigated in relation to age, gender, and type of sport, among other factors. Findings are relatively consistent in demonstrating that self-esteem for athletes is higher than for non-athletes. For instance, Hoganbruen developed a 4-week sports camp for young adolescent girls to determine the effect on self-esteem. Significant and positive changes in global self-esteem were found. Moreover, improved self-esteem contributed to the perception of personal competence. An increase in self-esteem nurtured through athletic competition assists middle school girls to cope with the negative influences and social turmoil experienced in their daily lives.

For adolescent girls, in particular, participation in sports has demonstrated an increase in self-esteem except for sports with rigid body type requirements (e.g., gymnastics). A girl who feels good about herself physically tends to present herself as a socially strong person. For example, the Women's Sports Foundation in U.S. has proposed that girls who have high self-esteem are less likely to become pregnant as teenagers and are more likely to leave an abusive relationship than girls with low self-esteem. High self-esteem is no guarantee that middle school girls will make the right decisions, but it provides a strong foundation, along with peer support of team members, for resisting many negative pressures.

Impressionable, athletic, middle school girls need positive and empowering role models to emulate while developing personal and interpersonal skills. Fortunately, coaches, officials, and parent volunteers are additional role models of leadership that student athletes are exposed to, compared to the general student body. In addition to the leaders in their daily lives, contemporary women athletes are the women that girls consider empowering leaders too.

Athletes such as Mia Hamm, Marion Jones, Rebecca Lobo, and Venus and Serena Williams surmounted obstacles and emerged as role models of leadership and athletic success.

Athletic participation and early leadership experiences may improve a girl's leadership skills. The initiative to lead is instilled through athletic achievement, competition, and self-confidence. Development of leadership ability through athletic competition was not the original intention of school districts offering interscholastic sports. However, the emerging connection between athletic participation and leadership skills may assist school personnel to intentionally incorporate leadership training for girls with athletic ability. Coaches and parent volunteers should work to develop leadership skills in adolescent girls with the support of school personnel.

Research supports that an early investment in leadership training can yield lifelong benefits for the athlete and society. In the spirit of No Child Left Behind, girls, regardless of athletic ability, may benefit from intentional leadership development. Although opportunities exist for the athlete to develop leadership skills, school personnel must not overlook the non-athletic girl. Traditionally, girls have had few formal opportunities to develop leadership skills. Girls should be encouraged to attend leadership seminars as well as participate in recreational sports and extracurricular activities in school and in the community. School personnel must prepare all girls to lead.

Censorship of School Guidance Materials

A challenge should not be equated with censorship. Some parents, for personal reasons, may request a school to provide alternative guidance materials or to have their children excused from certain guidance activities. Many schools will accommodate these requests. Censorship, however, is a main tactic of some national organisations that want to change the way schools select and use educational materials. Censorship, as defined by the American Library Association's Intellectual Freedom Committee, is the removal of material from open access by government authority. Censors try to impose their views by deciding what others should not read, see, or hear.

Special interests groups are trying to force many school systems to remove or alter developmental guidance materials and practices. The freedom of these groups to speak and write is guaranteed by the First Amendment; however, some of these groups are unwilling to grant such freedom to those who hold opposing views. Special interests groups are an essential ingredient in a democracy and contribute to the formation of public policy, but they can also be a negative and restrictive force. Few challenges by special interests groups reach the courts, but self-censorship happens. A group makes itself known and a counsellor silently retreats from the use of established materials and practices. The special interests group goes away and so do some developmentally-appropriate guidance materials.

Each year, People for the American Way, an organisation that is opposed to censorship, compiles a list of challenges to school textbooks and materials. This annual compilation includes attempts to remove guidance materials, library books, textbooks, films, and other instructional materials. A review of the four most recent annual reports indicates that a wide array of guidance materials have been challenged in various school districts throughout the United States. It is important to note that in the vast majority of cases where challenges have occurred, school boards have elected to retain and use the challenged materials.

An analysis of 53 recent challenges which occurred in 1988-1991 reveals that the following reasons were those most frequently cited by challengers:

- "New Age" concerns—hypnotism, self-hypnosis, meditation, Far East religions, guided fantasy, visualisation
- Undermining parental authority/family values and teaching children they can handle problems on their own
- Promoting secular humanism

Other reasons, "having teachers and untrained persons act as therapists," "having children harmed in some way because of exposure to certain material or practice," and "using materials unproven by research" seem to be emerging as three that challengers are citing more frequently.

The challengers have the right to challenge. If that opportunity does not exist, there is little reason for the First Amendment to exist. When public schools are involved, however, a number of pivotal issues become apparent. Items deemed by the state to be in the best interest of all students are not always acceptable to certain parents and special interests groups. Even after thorough adherence to materials selection policies, a school district that adopts a set of materials for counsellors to use in helping build self-esteem may find itself the subject of charges by selected parents and, in some cases, well-financed special interests groups. How can the rights of the many be protected and the rights of the minority be accommodated?

Parental and community involvement should be encouraged. At issue, here, is the notion that a small, vocal minority, often well-organised and well-financed by legal defence funds, can make it appear as though it represents the community as a whole. Group guidance and health education activities related to sex education and AIDS education have been opposed in certain communities. In some cases a small group of parents has requested the removal of a state- or locally-developed sex-education curriculum and requested that one which meets their criteria be substituted for the "offending" curriculum.

Should materials that have been selected on the basis of carefully-designed procedures and policies be altered, removed, or replaced when opposition by a few emerges? Not only has the use of certain developmental guidance materials been challenged, but the freedom to counsel in both individual and group settings has been questioned on occasion. Sometimes it is the use of materials which has caused certain groups to call for the removal of school counsellors. During the 1989-90 school year the Armstrong County Taxpayers League of Armstrong, Pennsylvania objected to some developmental guidance materials.

In addition to requesting the removal of guidance materials, the League campaigned to remove all guidance counsellors. Counsellors must assess whether they are functioning in an environment where the school board has a commitment to free expression or whether it is a board which placates a vocal minority. In some cases, counsellors may find themselves working with board members who have been elected with the support of special interests groups whose agendas include forcing their viewpoint on materials selection and curriculum practices.

To what extent are counsellors free to use certain materials that support the goals of the school without fear of retribution and, at the same time, to what extent do counsellors have support for designing alternative programmes to meet unique student and parental needs? Counsellors have sought ways to encourage students to sort out their own values. However, such activities become troublesome to certain parents who confuse values education with morality education. Many school personnel choose to avoid private morality topics, which they believe are better left to the home and church.

Some parents believe that religious beliefs and private morality issues should have a place in the school curriculum. The stated goal of several special interests groups is to bring public education under the control of Christians. The absence of references to religion by guidance materials and textbooks authors, counsellors, and teachers have brought accusations that the schools are in fact practicing religion—the religion of secular humanism. To what extent should private morality be addressed in the nation's public schools?

The pivotal issues surrounding challenges to school guidance materials and programmes can be further reduced to two very important questions that must be addressed if schools are to deal effectively with challenges to developmental guidance materials: (1) Who determines what school guidance materials are used in public schools? and (2) Is the role of schools seen primarily as a place where diverse ideas should be presented and explored or is the role of schools to be primarily that of transmitting community values?

Actions for Preventing Problems

Peterson and Poppen have developed a 16-item "Actions to Prevent Problems Checklist" which outlines steps that school districts and counsellors can take to prevent the likelihood that challenges will result in censorship. The 16 actions are not arranged in order of importance, but four may be of high priority for many counsellors:

- Base developmental guidance programming on sound educational practices which are appropriate for the age and maturity level of students.
- Relate developmental guidance goals and activities to district and state educational goals and to student educational needs.
- Ask the Board of Education to act on materials selection and materials reconsideration policies and procedures.
- Read "The School Counsellor and Censorship," the position statement of the American School Counsellor Association.

If challenges happen, responsible actions are needed by school counsellors:

- Listen carefully to those who express special concerns.
- Avoid debate, but do state the basis for current practices.
- Handle complaints with carefully constructed procedures and accurate records of all contact and actions.
- Keep the focus of the complaint on the material rather than on the programme.
- Ask for assistance from other district personnel, publishers (several publishers of "challenged" guidance materials have excellent printed materials for use in "challenge" situations), and professional associations.

Bibliography

Castricone, A. M., W. W. Finan, and S. K. Gumble, "Focus on Career Search: A Program for High School Students and Their Parents." *The School Counselor*, 1982.

Daniels, M. H., J. S. Karmos, and C. A. Presley, "Parents And Peers: Their Importance In The Career Decision Making Process". Carbondale, IL: Southern Illinois University, 1983.

Gerler, E. R., Drew, N. S., & Mohr, P., "Succeeding in middle school: A multimodal approach". *Elementary School Guidance and Counseling*, 1990.

______________., Hogan, C. C., & O'Rourke, K., "The challenge of counseling in middle schools". Ann Arbor, Michigan: ERIC/CAPS and The American School Counselor Association, 1990.

Hoyt, K. B., & Shylo, K. R., "Career education in transition: Trends and implications for the future". Columbus: ERIC Clearinghouse on Adult, Career, and Vocational Education, The Ohio State University, 1987.

______________., "Helping Parents Understand Career Education." *Journal Of Career Education*, 1984.

Laramore, D., "Parents' Role in the Education and Career Decision-making Process." *Journal Of Career Education*, 1984.

McDaniels, C. and D. Hummel, "Parents and Career Education." *Journal Of Career Education*, 1984.

Navin, S. L. and S. J. Sears, "Parental Roles in Elementary Career Guidance." *Elementary School Guidance And Counseling*, 1980.

Otto, L. B. and V. R. A. Call, "Parental Influence on Young People's Career Development." *Journal Of Career Development*, 1984.

_______________., "Bringing Parents Back In." *Journal Of Career Education*, 1984.

Smith, P. B., Nenny, S. W., & McGill, L., "Health problems and sexual activity of selected inner city, middle school students". *Journal of School Health*, 1986.

Splete, H., and A. Freeman-George, "Family Influences on Career Development of Young Adults." *Journal of Career Development*, 1985.

Welte, J. W., & Barnes, G. M., "Alcohol: The gateway to other drug use among secondary-school students". *Journal of Youth and Adolescence*, 1985.

Index